The
ABORTION
REVOLUTION

The ABORTION REVOLUTION

and the sanctity of human life

by Allen Quist

NORTHWESTERN PUBLISHING HOUSE
Milwaukee, Wisconsin

Library of Congress Catalog Card Number: 80-80874
Northwestern Publishing House
3624 W. North Ave., Milwaukee, Wis. 53208
©1980 by Northwestern Publishing House. All rights reserved
Published 1980
Printed in the United States of America
ISBN 0-8100-01152

CONTENTS

ACKNOWLEDGEMENTS

This is a book for which I shall take full responsibility but little credit. A study of the abortion question has hardly been one of my lifegoals and writing itself has always held little interest for me. But several years ago I became somewhat concerned about the rather obvious implications of the Supreme Court's *Roe v. Wade* decision of 1973 which legalized abortion. And since I teach in the area of human growth and development, I felt obligated to explore the decision's impact on the human development field. In my study I encountered the analyses of *Roe* as made by Harold O. J. Brown and as made by Paul Ramsey. Their critiques confirmed my own suspicions that the Court's ruling is only part of a large-scale revolution which is now occurring in our country, a revolution that is fast becoming, or already is, the most significant political, legal, and social change of our time.

Even so, the evident need for a greater public awareness of the destructive nature of the revolution was insufficient to compel me to write this work. In my college classes I could inform my students about the realities of what was happening; I was satisfied with that teaching role. But I will have to admit that sometimes the best teaching in my classes was done by the students. When they began to see what was involved in the revolution, they then began to press for a broader circulation of the basic facts. One student in particular, Robert Fleischmann (who is now enrolled in the seminary of the Wisconsin Evangelical Lutheran Synod), was especially instrumental in encouraging me to put this information into book form. He also contributed much of the research and many of the ideas which are incorporated in this book and additionally provided much-needed ongoing criticism of the work as it was progressing.

I would also like to recognize the invaluable assistance of my faithful wife Diane. Besides serving as proofreader, she has consistently supported and encouraged me in this effort. At the same time she has provided an inspiration to me by virtue of her own love and concern both for myself and for the millions of exploited infants in the world community.

Even our six children have supported my work — Emily, age twelve, who has unselfishly given of her time and talents to meet the pressing needs of our family so that I could more completely concentrate on research; Lisa, age ten, who has asked me more good questions about the abortion issue than any other student I have ever had; Laurie, age eight, whose gracious smile and demeaner have provided a constant reminder of the beauty and joy which are given in human life; Andrew, age six, whose quick mind has revealed over and over again the pressing need for the careful instruction of our nation's youth, especially with regard to moral values; Nathan, age three, whose zest for life and cooperative spirit have so often illustrated that individual well-being is a vital concern for the entire human family; and Katie, age 28 days, whose wondrous birth amply testifies to the awesome gift of life which God in his love has bestowed upon us, and whose vulnerable existence provides a sobering reminder of the millions of other infants who are now being deprived of life.

It is to these unnamed millions of the world that this book is dedicated.

Allen Quist
September 25, 1979

CHAPTER 1

THE LINES
OF BATTLE

In the *Chronicles of Narnia* by C. S. Lewis we read of a series of battles between the forces of evil and the forces of good. The forces of evil, as described by Lewis, have this common character-istic — to their own advantage they exploit and destroy innocent human beings. The forces of good have the opposite trademark — they seek to help and protect those persons who are vulnerable to the powers of evil. Since the forces of evil are unwilling to voluntarily cease their destructive deeds, and since the forces of good are willing to risk even their lives to protect the innocent, there inevitably results dramatic warfare between these two camps. These confrontations take many different forms and are fought on the battlegrounds of all the world's nations during every epoch of history. These battles will continue, suggests Lewis, until the last battle is silenced by the trumpet which signals the end of time.

In the United States of America there is at least one prominent front where the battle between good and evil is now intense. On this battlefield the forces of evil now have control and are destroy-ing many. Where evil is unrestrained, the plunder of the helpless is the order of the day. But men of good will are unwilling to sit passively by and watch the innocent being destroyed. The forces of good are actively working to regain the ground which has been lost. Meanwhile, the other side is trying to deeply entrench itself, intending to defy any and all offensives from the good. The outcome of this contest is by no means clear.

And what is this battle? A recent issue of *Time* headlines it as "The Fanatical Abortion Fight," which is characterized, says *Time*, by intense political confrontations and no compromise on either side.[1] Those who advocate abortion on demand have held the advantage for the past six years, the result being the deaths of millions of unborn infants. But, observes *Time,* "the momentum has swung to the pro-life group" which has produced "smashing legislative victories."[2] Yet, in spite of these victories, and because of the decisions of the United States Supreme Court beginning with *Roe v. Wade* 1973, the number of abortions has continued its dramatic increase. By 1977 the annual number of abortions in the U.S. had risen to 1,300,000,[3] an incredible seven-fold increase since 1970. This rate continues to rise.

As the strength of the pro-life forces builds, while at the same time the number of abortions escalates, the likelihood of a major battle steadily grows. Meanwhile, the killing of our unborn infants goes on — unchecked.

CHAPTER 2

THE SILENT TESTIMONY

In any war there are several smaller battles. One such clash occurred on February 15, 1979 in Washington D.C. This account of the confrontation was given by Carolyn Gerster, President of National Right to Life: Educational Foundations Incorporated Incorporated (reprinted by permission):

> Perhaps you read of the invitation from NOW (National Organization for Women) to meet together to discuss the formation of "comprehensive reproductive health programs." They made it clear that abortion itself would not be discussed. NOW's stated purpose was to "end the polarization and violence."
>
> Since the *violence of abortion* is the polarizing issue, however, most major pro-life groups agreed to refuse to meet unless the life issue was addressed. Those that did attend were undoubtedly motivated by the hope that positive programs might result from a dialogue with the pro-abortionists. We thought differently, however. We saw it as an attempt to cloud the central issue of abortion. We saw it as a devisive tactic.
>
> If our opponents could split off even a few pro-life groups our momentum might be slowed. If they could convince a few pro-life leaders to join with them in discussing peripheral issues, the realization of the Human Life Amendment might be delayed.
>
> The meeting was held on Thursday, February 15, in Washington D.C. All the pro-abortion groups and their leaders were there. A small group of pro-lifers did attend. The press waited outside until it was over. Every time the subject of abortion came up during the meeting the parlimentarian ruled it out of order. The time was largely spent discussing sex education and contraceptives for minors.

When it was over, it seemed as if the pro-abortionists had had their way. It apparently convinced a few pro-life individuals present that if they worked together on the above issues there would be fewer abortions. Unfortunately, it is a matter of record that up to now the opposite has been true. The pro-abortionists were attempting to use the meeting to obtain further concessions from Congress and to isolate the millions of the rest of us as extremists.

Four members of the Cleveland P.E.A.C.E. group (People Expressing a Concern for Everyone) attended the meeting for a different purpose. The young people did something that pulled the curtain away from the pro-abortion subterfuge before the press and showed to all where the real violence and polarization lay. During the meeting they did not disrupt the discussions. They waited. The meeting adjourned. The press was invited inside. The pro-abortionists began their statements about how there had been an amicable and productive discussion — how all had agreed on the need for education on the reproductive process and how they anticipated the beginning of co-operation between reasonable representative groups.

Then it happened.

Three young women walked to the center of the room and turned to face the group. One held a blue receiving blanket in her arms. Another spoke a simple statement: "Out of respect for NOW we came in good faith and not to disrupt this meeting. However, for those of us who love the unborn and for those who do not know the unborn, here is our sister killed by abortion." With this the young women pulled the receiving blanket aside to reveal a beautiful, perfectly formed tiny black girl. She had been killed by abortion.

There was a stunned silence as the young women continued: "The polarization and violence of the abortion issue which supposedly initiated this meeting was never touched upon. The issue of abortion was ignored and deliberately passed over in an attempt to deny the fact that indeed babies are dying. An entire group of our sisters was not represented here. These sisters were tragically and violently destroyed by abortion. The polarization and violence will not end until the American people recognize the dignity of this human life."

Pandemonium broke loose!

There was shock, shouting, tears. Everyone stood, some turned away visibly shaken. Some were angry. There were cameras, lights, flash blubs and in the midst stood the young woman holding the murdered little girl.

It was reported that an infamous East Coast abortionist leaped forward from his chair, said "Oh, my God," then sat back speechless. It was reported that the NOW people were really in tears as were several other pro-abortion leaders — whether from anger at the disruption of their plans or from the emotional shock, we will never know.

The tears in the eyes of some case-hardened reporters, however, were real. They had thought they had known all about abortion but now suddenly they were facing reality. Abortion was no longer an intellectual or political discussion for this murdered baby girl. Some reporters standing in that room wept openly.

There were those who were not converted, however. It was reported that a *New York Times* reporter was angry. He was asked: "Have you seen the baby?" and he replied: "Yes, I saw your baby and I don't ever want to see your — — baby again." Some denounced the action with words like "You betrayed us ... you destroyed us ... we're appalled by your action...." The truth was more than they could cope with.

The little baby girl could not say a word but as the noisy tumult swirled about her she had spoken louder and far more powerfully than anyone else at that carefully programmed meeting. The murdered body of one little girl had returned the focus to where it was to remain.

Let me tell you about this little girl. She had been killed two days earlier. She weighed approximately one pound and was seventeen weeks old when Upjohn's drug *prostaglandin* had caused her death by abortion.

There had been another tiny body, that of an older, four-pound baby girl killed by salt-poisoning on the same day. This larger baby was not shown because most of her skin had been burned by the corrosive effect of the salt. Her body was contracted and her face had been contorted in death.

These young people from P.E.A.C.E. had planned the protest in secret. They had hesitated several times. Was this the right thing to do? They discussed it. They prayed that this would help rather than discredit the pro-life movement. The night before in a hotel room, they told later, they had tenderly bathed the two tiny bodies. The younger baby had been christened Mary Elizabeth and the older Ruth. They had wrapped them carefully in receiving blankets that morning.

A day later there was a simple funeral. The clergyman read from the book of *Jeremiah*: "Before I formed you in the womb I knew you. Before you were born, I dedicated you."

CHAPTER 3

THE REVOLUTION

Those who advocate abortion often argue that women will have abortions anyway, whether it is legal or not. Even though there is a small grain of truth in such a statement, the position is highly misleading. There are many genuine evils that continue to plague mankind even though they are illegal. Robbery still occurs, as does rape, as does murder. But the fact that these ills persist, even though they are illegal, hardly suggests the laws prohibiting such acts should, therefore, be dropped. A primary function of government is the restraint of evil so that the innocent are protected. It is amazing that a legal and moral principle as basic as this could be so obscured in our day. Laws will never eliminate evil. But good laws can repress evil sufficiently so that civilization is possible.

Other abortion advocates have abandoned this former line of argument because they realized that to say women will have abortions regardless of the law is to admit that abortion is wrong. These spokesmen contend instead that women have a "right" to abortion. It is true that laws prohibiting abortion limit what women can legally do. But all laws limit what people can legally do. Is there a right to abortion? Our Constitution has never suggested that there is and the Hippocratic Oath, the long standing creed of the medical profession, expressly forbids abortion. The real concern for a democracy is not whether someone's so called freedom is being curtailed. The genuine concern is that all persons actually have those rights and freedoms which are essential to a free society. This means there is no such thing as a freedom or right which deprives another of his freedoms or rights. The denial of the rights of others is a mark of a totalitarian state. The equal protection by law of everyone's legitimate rights is *the mark* of a free state. As we will see, the abortion revolution is promoted under the guise of human rights, but the revolution is actually a key element in tyranny.

Because abortion is a genuine evil (except when used to save the mother's life), it must be legally restrained. Abortion is like an epidemic. While our nation had the moral strength to oppose it, the practice of abortion was more or less held in check. But since abortion on demand has been legalized, the procedure has spread like a plague throughout each of the fifty states to become our nation's number one cause of death (assuming that abortion takes the life of a human being; a thesis which will be demonstrated beyond reasonable doubt in chapter five).

The results of the abortion revolution are shocking. Today in our land better than one baby out of every four is killed by abortion prior to birth. This rate is rapidly approaching one out of every three. The life expectancy of a person born alive in our country is about 72 years. The life expectancy of a person conceived in our country, should his mother elect for abortion, is about 72 days. But as terrible as this situation is now, it is only a beginning of what may well occur in the years to come. Romania, a country which has had permissive abortion laws for a number of years, "terminates" 80 per cent of its conceived infants through abortion.[4] Japan now terminates 70 per cent.[5]

HOW ABORTION BECAME LEGAL
IN THE UNITED STATES

Before 1970 all fifty states had laws prohibiting abortion under most circumstances, the exception being the rare case of its use to save the mother's life. (The states have always recognized the sad necessity of sacrificing the unborn infant's life when required to avoid losing the lives of both mother and child.) In the late 1960s, however, ten states adopted laws which would also permit abortion in the instance of protecting the mother's mental health, or if the child would be born with grave defects, or if the pregnancy resulted from rape or incest. These new laws followed the guidelines suggested by the American Law Institute in 1962 and by the American Medical Institute in 1967.[6]

But even with this relaxing of the laws in the 1960s, in 1969 there were still only 22,670 legal abortions.[7] There were also illegal abortions of course; but judging from the low number of maternal deaths due to abortion, there could not have been many illegal procedures.[8] Even so, the abortion revolution had actually begun; because, if you can justify abortion for reasons of mental health, you can justify it for any reason whatsoever.

The actual practice of abortion on demand began in 1970 when the states of New York, Washington, Hawaii and Alaska adopted highly permissive abortion laws. In these states a woman had only to request an abortion by the fourth to the sixth month of pregnancy (depending on the state) and she could legally have it done for no additional reason. New York adopted the most permissive law, allowing for abortion during the first six months of pregnancy with no requirement that the woman be a resident of the state. As a result of this liberal law, New York City soon became our nation's abortion capital with some 600,000 abortions being done during the first 30 months of the law's effect.[9] Apparently the majority of the women involved were from out of state.[10] When, in 1971, the New York legislature realized the disastrous effect its new law was having, it reversed itself by passing a bill to rescind the permissive law. Unfortunately, Nelson Rockefeller, who was then governor, vetoed the bill to rescind and the law stood.

The pro-abortion factions exerted political pressure upon the legislatures of other states to adopt similar laws. These efforts were unsuccessful however, and in 1971 and 1972 there were no other states that followed the trend toward open abortion laws. In 1972 North Dakota and Michigan held referendums to determine the public's view of the new trend. The permissive laws were soundly defeated in both states. The margins of defeat were two to one in Michigan, three to one in North Dakota. Nevertheless, the protective laws in the majority of states had been effectively undercut by the liberal laws in four states, especially by the law in New York; because a pregnant woman could just travel to a permissive state in order to have an abortion.

Realizing that further political gains were now being stymied, the abortion proponents turned their attentions to the courts. It was in this arena that the abortionists won their big victory — on January 22, 1973, in *Roe v. Wade* the United States Supreme Court decreed that almost all state laws which prohibited abortion were "unconstitutional." After this landmark decision most states found themselves with no significant protection for the unborn's right to live. The revolution was now complete; abortion on demand became the legal practice in every state of the union.

Specifically the Court ruled that the states could neither regulate nor prohibit abortion in the first trimester (three months) of pregnancy; that the states could regulate but not prohibit abortion in the second trimester; and that the states could both regulate and prohibit abortion in the last trimester, except when the procedure was deemed necessary to preserve the life or health of the mother. At first it appeared that the Court would at least allow for the infant's protection during the time of "viability" (the supposed point after six months when the "fetus" can live without his mother), but even this protection was later destroyed by the Court in *Doe v. Bolton*. In this companion decision to *Roe* the Court ruled that the mother's health must be interpreted in its broadest possible meaning and must include psychological, emotional, familial and other factors. The result of these two decisions is that American women can now get abortions right up to the moment of birth.

THE RESULTS OF LEGALIZED ABORTION

The loss of legal protection for our unborn infant's right to live has had catastrophic consequences, especially with regard to the number of abortions being done. The following chart describes the relationship between the destruction of the protective laws and the resulting destruction of infant lives:[11]

ANNUAL LEGAL ABORTIONS IN THE U.S.

1969	22,670
1970	193,500
1971	485,500
1972	586,500
1973	744,600
1974	898,600
1975	1,084,200
1976	1,179,300
1977	1,270,000

There are several deeply troubling truths which are evident from these statistics. In the first place, the total number of abortions — more than six million in this decade already — is an atrocity of major proportions. Secondly, the continuous upward trend in the number of abortions strongly suggests that the practice will continue to mushroom. (Is there any reason to believe that our nation's experience will be any different from that of Romania and Japan?) And thirdly, the direct relationship between legalization and the rapid increase in abortions done is simply obvious from the figures.

There are many reasons why the frequency of abortion expands rapidly under legalization. Among these reasons are the values which accompany abortion — the practice carries with it a reduced appreciation for children, a loss of regard for sexual morality and large scale reliance on abortion as a means of birth control. A hedonistic pursuit of pleasure and denial of responsibility are other marks of the abortion culture. The history of many countries has proven these things to be true. Perhaps it would be well for us as a nation to take a hard look down the roller-coaster path we are traveling. Is this really the kind of state we wish to be in?

Another concern for our country is the consequence the revolution has had on our birth rate. The following chart summarizes the impact:[12]

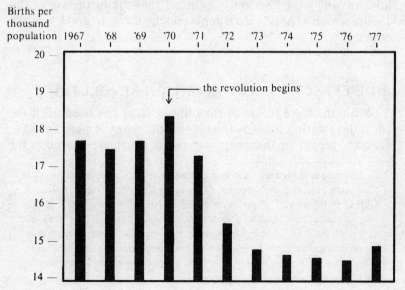

BIRTH RATES OF THE UNITED STATES

From these figures we can see that the birth rate made a moderate upswing after reaching a low point in 1968; but in 1970 the abortion rate began its dramatic increase and the birth rate plummeted proportionately. We might keep in mind that the advocates of permissive abortion often claim that women were having abortions already, and that liberal laws have simply allowed them to get abortions legally. The striking plunge in our birth rate, which just happens to coincide perfectly with the abortion revolution, demonstrates how totally false this pro-abortion argument is.

Some individuals might be so foolhardy as to suggest that this low birth rate is a good thing. The error in such a position is quickly seen when we consider that the birth rate of the 1960s was just above the replacement level, the birth rate needed to maintain a stable population over the normal life span of 72 years. The replacement level birth rate for North America is now 17.5 births per thousand population.* But, as we can see from the chart, the birth rate of the 1970s is way below replacement level. (The total number of births per year can be obtained by multiplying the births per thousand times our population of 220,000,000. We now have about 3,300,000 births per year, while in the 1960s we had about 4,000,000 births per year.) It would be difficult to see how anyone would seriously contend that the birth rate of the 1970s, which is way below replacement level, is good for our country.

SIDE-EFFECTS OF THE ABORTION REVOLUTION

While the right to life of the unborn baby has been dealt the most devastating blow by the revolution, many Americans have failed to recognize that their own rights which are related to the

---

* 17.5 births per thousand is shown to equal the replacement level birth rate for North America in Nortman, "Changing Contraceptive Patterns: A Global Perspective," *Population Bulletin*, No. 3, August 1977, p. 32. "Replacement level birth rate" and "zero population growth rate" are used as synonyms in this book. This rate occurs when the average number of reproducing daughters born to a woman of reproductive age is equal to one. Other factors, such as wars or immigration can either lower or raise the actual population.

abortion issue have been seriously curtailed as well. For example, the rights of the individual states have been impaired by the Court's usurping the state's rightful role of deciding how the lives of the unborn are best protected and how the unborn's rights relate to the rights of others. Before *Roe v. Wade* it was the concern of each state to determine what the laws governing abortion should be. *Roe* stripped the states of that right and left them little room for enacting significant laws.

To make matters worse, in *Planned Parenthood v. Danforth,* 1976, and in *Belloti v. Baird,* 1979, the Court struck down state laws requiring parental consent for abortions done on teenage girls who are still minors. The 1976 decision also mandated that states could not require the approval of the woman's husband and/or the child's father before an abortion was done. Consequently, today pregnant teenage girls get abortions with neither the knowledge nor consent of their parents, and wives get abortions with neither the knowledge nor consent of their husbands, normally the child's father. What kind of justice is this? In the name of women's rights the Court has seriously reduced the rights of all fifty states, has restricted the rights of parents, has destroyed the right and duty of fathers to protect their own unborn sons and daughters and has refused to recognize the husband as having a significant voice in the abortion decision. Is this equal rights under the law? Or is this despotism? We should begin to see the truth of the principle that ultimately our rights are protected only when everyone's rights are protected. To plunder one of us is to plunder us all.

CHAPTER 4

THE REASONING
OF THE SUPREME COURT

The *Roe v. Wade* ruling of the Supreme court amazed even the pro-abortion forces. After all, every one of the fifty states possessed laws regulating abortion, most of those laws being highly protective of the unborn infant's life. These statutes had been scrutinized, debated, amended and passed by thousands of elected legislators and had been signed by hundreds of elected governors. Some of these laws had been in effect for over one hundred years. If all these laws were actually unconstitutional, why had not these thousands of public officials even suspected that such might be the case?

With the exception of the past few years, the laws had been progressing toward tighter restrictions on abortion, the reason being that medical knowledge was making it increasingly certain that the unborn was a living human being. As early as 1859, for example, the American Medical Association passed resolutions urging the states to enact laws which would protect the unborn infant from the earliest stages of pregnancy onward because of, as stated by the A.M.A., "the independent and actual existence of the child before birth as a living being."[13] How could the Court see fit to destroy these life-protecting laws?

In defense of its decree the Court said that a pregnant woman has a "right to privacy" and this right overrules any rights the unborn child might have. And how can a right to privacy outweigh another's right to live? The Court assumed that unborn babies are not included in the Constitution's definition of "persons," therefore, said the Court, the mother's rights take precedence over the baby's.

The complete bankruptcy of this reasoning by the Court is easy to see. In the first place, the right to privacy can not reasonably include the abortion decision. Abortion is not done in private; it is carried out in public hospitals and clinics. Furthermore, abortion is performed by doctors having no personal ties with the mother; it is assisted by nurses working in their chosen profession; it is often paid for by public money; and it is subject to various governmental standards and reports. This is all a far cry from the refuge of one's own bedroom, to which the right to privacy properly applies. (But even in our own home we are legally and morally prohibited from harming someone else.) When the Supreme court chose the right of privacy upon which to base its decision, it was simply reaching for straws. There is nothing in our Constitution which in any way suggests a right of abortion. (Technically, the Court said that the abortion decision was to be made between the woman and her doctor, but actually the woman decides and the physician merely provides the services.)

In the second place, the Court said the Fourteenth Amendment (which guarantees equal protection under the law and the right to life for all persons) does not necessarily apply to unborn infants. This position is ludicrous — the Fourteenth Amendment was enacted at the very time when states were actively extending their anti-abortion laws.[14] It is totally inconceivable that the Congress which passed the fourteenth Amendment and the states which ratified it were excluding unborn babies.

In the third place, and most importantly, the Court simply closed its eyes to the fact that the unborn are living human beings. Because this is the most important reality behind good laws regulating abortion, the next chapter will concentrate on this one truth.

But at this point the following conclusion is clear: It is all too evident that the Supreme Court was not actually interpreting the Constitution, which is its only legal function. Instead the Court was writing radical new legislation — legislation which would put the Court itself into the forefront of the abortion revolution. Any possible doubt that this conclusion is correct should be removed by the newly published study of the Supreme Court's recent history called *The Brethren*. The authors, Woodward and Armstrong, describe the final drafts of the *Roe v. Wade* majority opinion in this fashion:

> The clerks in most chambers were surprised to see the Justices, particularly Blackmun, so openly brokering their deci-

sion like a group of legislators. There was a certain reasonableness to the draft, some of them thought, but it derived more from medical and social policy than from constitutional law. There was something embarrassing and dishonest about this whole process. It left the Court claiming that the Constitution drew certain lines at trimesters and viability. The Court was going to make a medical policy and force it on the states. As a practical matter, it was not a bad solution. As a constitutional matter, it was absurd.[15]

Should it be any wonder that so many constitutional experts referred to the Court's ruling with terms like "without principle," "a failure," "a refusal of the Court's own discipline," "a transgression of all limits," "naked political preference," "comprehensive legislation," "beyond the outer limits of authority" and "a bad decision"?[16] Summarizing his own analysis of the Roe ruling, John Noonen, law professor at the University of California — Berkeley, stated flatly: "Scholarly authority judged the liberty to lack constitutional basis."[17] The establishment of the abortion right had been, as Justice White correctly observed in his dissenting opinion, "an act of raw judicial power."

CHAPTER 5

ARE UNBORN BABIES PERSONS?

The Supreme Court refused to recognize the rights of the unborn because they are not, said the Court, persons under the meaning of the Fourteenth Amendment. We will acknowledge that the Constitution gives no definition of the word "person," but why should a definition be given? The plain meaning of "person" is living human being. The medical-embryological facts, which the Court ignored, leave no room for doubt regarding the humanity of the unborn baby. To demonstrate this truth, let us consider several statements from recent textbooks dealing with human embryology (books that have no pro-life bias). One such statement acknowledges the following:

> The fetal period of development is from about the eighth week, when the embryo becomes a recognizable human being. (1979 edition of *Human Development: the Span of Life*)[18]

We perhaps should note that about half of all abortions occur after the eighth week. Another similar statement is:

> By the end of the embryonic period, [eight weeks] the organism is clearly human . . . (1979 edition of *Developmental Psychology Today*)[19]

The basic details of prenatal development are described in the following longer quotation:

> *The Fetal Stage.* After the eighth week or so the embryo is called a *fetus.* It is now about 2½ inches long and weighs about an ounce, but has advanced so far along the road to birth that it needs a new name. The fetus is essentially a miniature baby, with a heart, lungs, brain, spinal cord, sense organs, face and even stubby fingers and toes. Only a few parts of the body remain to be differentiated such as the external sex organs and the nails of the fingers and toes. It needs to grow much more

and to refine its structures, but the major process during this period is for the fetus' body to learn how to use and coordinate all the intricate and delicate equipment it has been building during the embryonic period.

Some highlights of fetal development during the next seven months are these:

Third month.   In this month the fetus begins to show signs that it is not only human but an individual. Distinctive physical characteristics can be observed in body shape and structures. Fetal activity increases in which individual differences can be noted. Respiratory movements have been reported, and urea has been detected in the amniotic fluid indicating kidney functioning.

Fourth month.   The fetus is now about 9 inches tall, having reached half the height it will have at birth. The entire reproductive system has been formed. The repertoire of activities includes thumb sucking, hiccuping, and all the reflexes found in the normal newborn infant except for vocal responses and functional respiration. Almost all the body's surface is sensitive to tactile stimulation. For example, it will curl its fingers when its palm is tickled and it will curl its toes when it is tickled on the soles of its feet.

Fifth month.   The fetus is now about a foot long and weighs about a pound. Its movements by the end of this period can be real kicks. Because it is floating around in its fluid-filled sac, the fetus has marvelous ease and variety of movements. Sometimes it lies on one side and then on the other, sometimes it floats with its head down and sometimes with it up. By this time the fetus may have developed favorite positions and activities. The variability of fetal movements is marked. Some are noticeably active 75 per cent of the time, whereas others are active only occasionally.

Seventh month.   Fetuses born during this period have a fair chance for survival but only with tender care. The fetus has already acquired some immunities and some fat for warmth in preparation for the outside world, and its nervous system is sufficiently developed for independent functioning. The rate of fetal activity will increase until the final month when the snug fit in the uterus will limit freedom of movement.

Eighth and ninth months.   During this period the fetus begins to look more and more like a full-term baby. The fetus is making the final preparations for this first major trip. Its hair is longer; its nails grow beyond the tips of its fingers and toes; its repertoire of responses is practically complete.[20]

To enable us to picture the actual size of the developing infant, the following chart with quotation is included:

GROWTH OF THE HUMAN EMBRYO,[21] NATURAL SIZE

Growth from one-celled fertilized egg´ is rapid; by 18 days a head process is microscopically visible. A 5-week embryo has arm and leg buds; by 9 weeks these features have basically human shape. Fetus at 11 weeks, although less than 3 inches long, is obviously human in form.

 14 days

18 days

24 days

4 weeks

6 weeks

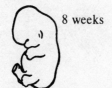 8 weeks

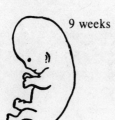 9 weeks

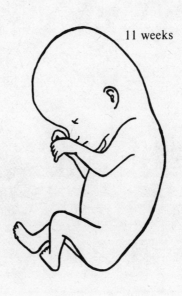 11 weeks

INCHES 0

1

2

3

4

The following sketches provide additional detail on the visual appearance of the unborn human being. (The drawings are courtesy of Elisa Boniek. They are not life-size.)

Six and one-half weeks

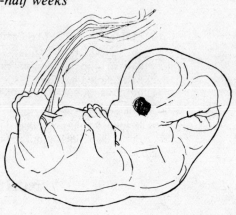

Eight weeks

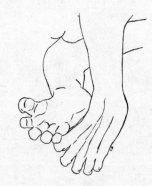

Twelve weeks

Sixteen weeks

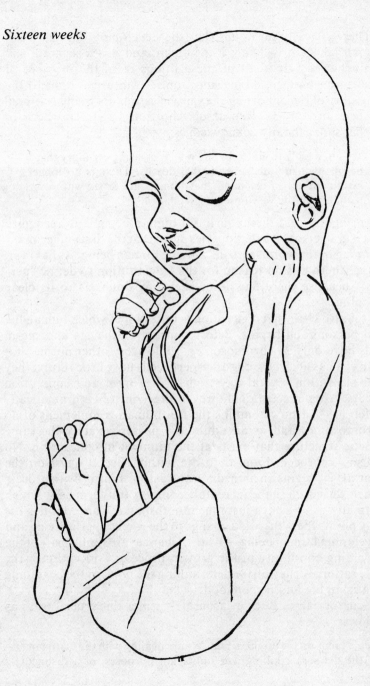

There is really no doubt that the developing organism is a human being. It is living; it is human; and it is a separate and distinct entity. It is all of these things from the moment of conception onward. Many abortionists will even admit to the humanity of the unborn. For example, a founder of the National Association for the Repeal of Abortion Laws, Dr. Bernard Nathanson, candidly acknowledges:

> I am deeply troubled by my own increasing certainty that I had in fact presided over 60,000 deaths. There is no longer serious doubt in my mind that human life exists within the womb from the very onset of pregnancy.[22]

To recognize that the unborn is a human being is to recognize that it is a person. All dictionaries agree that the first and primary meaning of the word "person" is living human being. As has been noted, there was no reason for the Constitution to define "person," because there has never been any doubt as to its clear meaning.

It is also clear that conception is the point at which human life and personhood begins. Before conception the egg and sperm cells have only 23 chromosomes, while every other normal human cell has 46. These egg and sperm cells have little future; they will die within several days unless they meet and conception occurs. After conception, however, the living cell is dramatically different — it now contains the full human complement of 46 chromosomes and as an adult will possess exactly the same genetic structure that exists at the moment of conception. No longer is the cell doomed to die within several days; on the contrary, it begins an immediate and astonishing growth process which will result in the incredibly complex full-term baby which normally will be born just nine months later. Conception is the only point where there is a change in the essence of the living and developing human being. All other changes are simply part of the unfolding continuity of the growth process. Conception is the only rational criterion for determining the point of the beginning of human life and personhood.

Senator James Buckley accurately states this crucial truth as follows:

> ... focus on the essential fact. We are dealing with the matter of the deliberate killing, for utilitarian purposes, of a distinct

human life that is biologically distinguishable from other human life only in that it has not as yet been born. We are dealing, in other words, not with "a part of the mother's body," but rather with a unique, genetically complete human being that until birth is sheltered and fed by the mother.[23]

Buckley's conclusion is inescapable; unborn human infants are persons and the United States of America is now engaged in the wholesale killing of innocent human beings.

34

CHAPTER 6

THE PRACTICE OF
ABORTION

The word "abortion" means to expel the fetus from the womb before it is viable. But since it is nature's intention that the developing organism should live and grow, this expulsion can only be done in a violent fashion. The procedure must of necessity override the protective framework of the mother's own body in order to succeed. It goes without saying that abortion is a totally unnatural (or contrary to nature) act.

Most abortions are done during the first trimester. By the end of this three month period the infant's heart has already been beating for eight weeks; the infant's brain has been active for six weeks (perhaps even earlier, but brain waves can be detected at six weeks). He has been moving about for some time; the mother would soon be able to notice those movements. During this trimester the abortionist uses the D and C technique (dilation and curettage) or the newer and more common "vacuum aspiration" which is a suction D and C. The abortionist's procedure is to force open the cervix (opening of the womb) and insert either a curette or suction tube. With this tool he tears the infant to pieces and removes the remains. Needless to say, the women are generally not shown these remains, because if they were, they would have real difficulty denying that it was a baby which had just been killed.

The most common form of second trimester abortion is the saline solution, also called "salting out." The abortionist inserts a hypodermic needle into the uterus (womb) and withdraws some of the amniotic fluid which surrounds and protects the infant. The abortionist then replaces the fluid with a salt solution. Since the baby has been breathing the amniotic fluid in and out of his lungs for some time, he now breathes in the salt solution as well which effectively poisons him. Because these babies, when delivered some hours or days later, are typically blistered and burned red from the salt, they are sometimes called "cherry-apple" babies. Several years ago the State of Missouri banned this procedure, but the U.S. Supreme Court (*Planned Parenthood v. Danforth*) ruled the Missouri law to be unconstitutional on the grounds that the saline technique is the most common form of second trimester abortion in other states.

Hysterotomy is the method of third trimester abortion. The word "hysterotomy" means to open the uterus, as opposed to "hysterectomy" which means to remove the uterus. Hysterotomy is exactly the same as childbirth by Caesarean section (named after the delivery of Julius Caesar) — with one vital difference. In a Caesarean section the objective is to save the child's life as well as the mother's, but in hysterotomy the goal is to kill the child. This is accomplished by clamping the umbilical chord shut before removing the baby from the mother's body. After suffocation has occurred, the now-dead baby is legally removed and disposed of. Can there be any doubt but that this action is nothing less than first degree murder? Can there be any doubt that all on demand abortions are first degree murder?

Today the only legal criterion for determining whether a baby can be killed is his location — inside the womb he can be killed at any time and for no justifiable reason, outside the womb he must be protected at all cost. This is the most superficial and arbitrary criterion conceivable, yet the infant's life or death hangs on this irrational guideline. This principle is changing somewhat, however. A recent Supreme Court decision suggests that infants who survive abortion can be legally allowed to die, since the intent of the operation was to kill the baby (*Beal v. Franklin,* 1979).

What is it like to have an abortion? The following personal testimony is included to give the reader some awareness of one woman's experience. You will notice that the account is both factual and impressionistic, but it is not exaggerated or overly dramatic. Keep in mind also that the first trimester abortion, as is described here, is the least horrifying of the current techniques. This account was printed in the *Minneapolis Tribune* on Saturday, May 29, 1976:

THERE JUST WASN'T ROOM IN OUR LIVES NOW
FOR ANOTHER BABY
By Jane Doe

New York

We were in a bar on Lexington Av. when I told my husband I was pregnant. It is not a memory I like to dwell on. Instead of the champagne and hope which heralded the impending births of our first, second and third children, the news of this one was greeted with shocked silence and Scotch. "Jesus," my husband kept saying to himself, stirring the ice cubes around and around. "Oh, Jesus."

Oh how we tried to rationalize it that night as the starting time for the movie came and went. My husband talked about his plans for a career change in the next year, to stem the staleness that 14 years with the same investment-banking firm had brought him. A new baby would preclude that option.

The timing wasn't right for me either. Having juggled pregnancies and child care with what freelance jobs I could fit in between feedings, I had just taken o a full-time job. A new baby would put me right back in the nursery just when our youngest child was finally school age. It was time for us, we tried to rationalize. There just wasn't room in our lives now for another baby. We both agreed. And agreed. And agreed.

How very considerate they are at the Women's Services, known formally as the Center for Reproductive and Sexual Health. Yes indeed. I could have an abortion that very Saturday morning and be out in time to drive to the country that afternoon. Bring a first-morning urine specimen, a sanitary belt and napkins, a money order or $125 cash — and a friend.

My friend turned out to be my husband, standing awkwardly and ill at ease as men always do in places that are exclusively for women, as I checked in at 9 a.m. Other men hovered around just as anxiously, knowing they had to be there, wishing they weren't. No one spoke to each other. When I would be cycled out of there four hours later, the same men would be slumped in their same seats, locked downcast in their cells of embarrassment.

The Saturday morning women's group was more dispirited than the men's in the waiting room. There were around 15 of us, a mixture of races, ages and backgrounds. Three didn't speak English at all, and a fourth, a pregnant Puerto Rican girl around 18, translated for them.

There were six black women and a hodge-podge of whites, among them a T-shirted teenager who kept leaving the room to throw up and a puzzled middle-aged woman from Queens with three grown children.

"What form of birth control were you using?" the volunteer asked each one of us. The answer was inevitably "none." She then went on to describe the various forms of birth control available at the clinic and offered them to each of us.

The youngest Puerto Rican girl was asked through the interpreter which she'd like to use: the loop, diaphragm or pill. She shook her head "no" three times. "You don't want to come back here again, do you?" the volunteer pressed. The girl's head was so low her chin rested on her breastbone. "Si," she whispered.

We had been there two hours by that time, filling out endless forms, giving blood and urine, receiving lectures. But unlike any other group of women I've been in, we didn't talk. Our common denominator, the one which usually floods across language and economic barriers into familiarity, today was one of shame. We were losing life that day, not giving it.

The group kept getting cut back to smaller, more workable units, and finally I was put in a small waiting room with just two other women. We changed into paper bathrobes and paper slippers, and we rustled whenever we moved. One of the women in my room was shivering, and an aide brought her a blanket.

"What's the matter?" the aide asked her. "I'm scared," the woman said. "How much will it hurt?" The aid smiled. "Oh nothing worse than a couple of bad cramps," she said. "This afternoon you'll be dancing a jig."

I began to panic. Suddenly the rhetoric, the abortion marches I'd walked in, the telegrams sent to Albany to counteract the Friends of the Fetus, the Zero Population Growth buttons I'd worn peeled away, and I was all alone with my microscopic baby. There were just the two of us there, and soon, because it was more convenient for me and my husband, there would be one again.

How could it be that I, who am so neurotic about life that I step over bugs rather than on them, who spend hours planting flowers and vegetables in the spring even though we rent out the house and never see them, who make sure the children are vaccinated and inoculated and filled with vitamin C, could so arbitrarily decide that this life shouldn't be?

38

"It's not a life," my husband had argued, more to convince himself than me. "It's a bunch of cells smaller than my fingernail."

But any woman who has had children knows that certain feeling in her taut, swollen breasts and the light but constant ache in her uterus that signals the arrival of a life. Though I would march myself into blisters for a woman's right to exercise the option of motherhood, I discovered there in the waiting room that I was not the modern woman I thought I was.

When my name was called, my body felt so heavy the nurse had to help me into the examining room. I waited for my husband to burst through the door and yell "Stop," but of course he didn't. I concentrated on three black spots in the acoustic ceiling until they grew in size to the shape of saucers, while the doctor swabbed my insides with antiseptic.

"You're going to feel a burning sensation now," he said, injecting Novocain into the neck of the womb. The pain was swift and severe, and I twisted to get away from him. He was hurting my baby, I reasoned, and the black saucers quivered in the air. "Stop," I cried. "Please stop." He shook his head, busy with his equipment. "It's too late to stop now," he said, "It'll just take a few more seconds."

What good sports we women are. And how obedient. Physically the pain passed even before the hum of the machine signals that the vacuuming of my uterus was completed, my baby sucked up like ashes after a cocktail party. Ten minutes from start to finish. And I was back on the arm of the nurse.

There were twelve beds in the recovery room. Each one had a gaily flowered draw sheet and a soft green or blue thermal blanket. It was all very feminine. Lying on these beds for an hour or more were the shocked victims of their sex life, their full wombs now stripped clean, their futures less encumbered.

It was very quiet in that room. The only voice was that of the nurse, locating the new women who had just come in so she could monitor their blood pressure and checking out the recovered women who were free to leave.

Juice was being passed about, and I found myself sipping a Dixie cup of Hawaiian Punch. An older woman with tightly curled bleached hair was just getting up from the next bed. "That was no goddamn snap," she said, resting before putting on her miniskirt and high white boots. Other women came and went, some walking out as dazed as they had entered, others with a bounce that signaled they were going right back to Bloomingdale's.

Finally, then, it was time for me to leave. I checked out, making an appointment to return in two weeks for an IUD insertion. My husband was slumped in the waiting room, clutching a single yellow rose wrapped in a wet paper towel and stuffed into a Baggie.

We didn't talk the whole way home, but just held hands very tightly. At home there were more yellow roses and a tray in bed for me and the children's curiosity to divert.

It had certainly been a successful operation. I didn't bleed at all for two days, just as they had predicted, and then I bled only moderately for another four days. Within a week my breasts had subsided and the tenderness vanished, and my body felt mine again instead of the eggshell it becomes when it's protecting someone else.

My husband and I are back to planning our summer vacation and his career switch.

And it certainly does make more sense not to be having a baby right now — we say that to each other all the time. But I have this ghost now. A very little ghost that only appears when I'm seeing something beautiful, like the full moon on the ocean last weekend. And the baby waves at me. And I wave at the baby. "Of course, we have room," I cry to the ghost. "Of course we do."[24]

Although this is a small consolation, at least "Jane Doe" went to a clinic that apparently practiced medically "safe" procedures. (We will see later that no abortion is really safe.) Many other women have been less fortunate. The financial attraction for becoming an abortionist is considerable and many practitioners have really cashed in by setting up assembly line techniques that make possible maximum profits. We can get some idea of what has been happening in such clinics by means of the recent news headlines from the *Chicago Sun Times* which reflect on the paper's investigation of several shoddy clinics in the area of Chicago. Several headlines read as follows:

"The abortion profiteers"
(11/12/78 issue of the *Sun Times*)

"Making a killing in Michigan Av. Clinics"
(11/12/78)
"Life on the abortion assembly line: Grim"
(11/12/78)
"Jury subpenas records of abortion clinic"
(11/12/78)
"Life on abortion assembly line: grisly, greedy"
(11/12/78)
"Men who profit from women's pain"
(11/13/78)
"Hot line credo: Get patient's money first"
(11/17/78)
"12 dead after abortions in state's walk-in clinics"
(11/19/78)
"Abortion mills in huge kickback scheme"
(11/19/78)
"Pregnant or not, women given abortions"
(11/19/78)
"Abortion counselor's job: sell, sell, sell"
(11/19/78)

The news stories which followed these headlines strongly suggest
that the headlines were not exaggerated. The abortionists had no
regard for the welfare of the mothers. Consequently, many of the
women were seriously injured and a number of them died. In
addition the clinics were defrauding the government out of many
thousands (perhaps millions) of tax dollars — money used to pay
for these "terminations of pregnancy." The abortion revolution
has made this corruption possible. Are such atrocities a danger
signal, perhaps, of the direction our nation is taking?

It is possible that these and other abortion clinics will soon be
obsolete, due to the availability of drugs that produce abortions
during the earliest stages of pregnancy so that no medical supervi-
sion would be necessary. On an experimental basis such drugs
already exist. Some of these would be taken by a woman after
missing a menstrual period "just to be safe." The drug would
produce an abortion if she is pregnant and this would happen at a
time when the woman would not even know for sure if she had
had an abortion or not. The action of the "morning after pill"
would be similar; the difference being that the woman would take

the drug after intercourse, again "just to be safe." Both types of drugs are actually abortifacients because they would destroy a human life after conception has occurred.

There is one other abortion producing device which we should be aware of and that is the IUD (intra-uterine device). Although commonly listed as a "contraceptive," this devise apparently affects the uterus in such a way as to prevent the conceived life from attaching itself to the uterine lining for nourishment. If this is actually how the IUD works (there is some debate on this matter), then it is actually producing abortions. (To avoid this problem there is a new trend for defining conception as the implantion, rather than the union, of the egg and sperm. But changing the definitions of words in no way affects what is really happening.) The other common types of contraceptives do actually prevent conception from happening and are not, therefore, abortifacients.

THE LANGUAGE OF ABORTION

Because the killing of human babies is so totally disgusting to most people, the abortion culture has successfully hid much of its practice through the use of euphemistic language (using acceptable words to denote unacceptable truths). Perhaps the most devastating euphemism of our day is the word "fetus." *Roe v. Wade,* for example, consistently avoids using words like "unborn baby" and uses instead the word "fetus." But what is a fetus? "Fetus" is the Latin word for unborn baby. Martin Luther knew the importance of avoiding Latin and using the common language so that people could understand what was being said. The abortionists know the value of using the Latin so that people are ignorant of what is being said (and done). Did you ever hear a pregnant woman say she felt her "fetus" moving? This book generally avoids the word "fetus" because it obscures the real nature of abortion. It is unborn human beings (we call them "babies" and "infants") that are being killed. Let us tell it like it is.

Another favorite euphemism is "termination of pregnancy." But again, this is not how we commonly speak. A pregnancy is also terminated when a child is born, but then we call it the birth of a baby. The only real difference between childbirth and abortion is that in abortion the child is deliberately killed.

One of the most honest commentaries on the euphemisms of the abortion culture was printed in *California Medicine* several years ago. The pro-abortion author states:

> Since the old ethic has not yet been fully displaced it has been necessary to separate the idea of abortion from the idea of killing, which continues to be socially abhorrent. The result has been a curious avoidance of the scientific fact, which everyone really knows, that human life begins at conception and is continuous whether intra- or extra-uterine until death. The very considerable semantic gymnastics which are required to rationalize abortion as anything but taking a human life would be ludicrous if they were not often put forth under socially impeccable auspices. It is suggested that this schizophrenic sort of subterfuge is necessary because while a new ethic is being accepted the old one has not yet been rejected.[25]

From these statements we can also see how successful the abortionists have been in hiding their atrocities. Perhaps it is time for the American public to face the stark realities of the abortion revolution. Perhaps a place to begin is by talking about the truth of what is really happening.

THE REASONS FOR
ABORTION

The advocates of permissive abortion laws have many arguments by which they hope to defend their position. Since none of these reasons provide an adequate rationale for abortion, a large number of arguments is required in order to confuse the minds of the American public. Let us consider these arguments one at a time, hoping to understand each of them clearly.

ABORTION MAY BE NECESSARY TO SAVE
THE MOTHER'S LIFE.

Although this statement may have some truth to it, this reason lends no support to the abortion revolution. In the first place, abortion for this reason is extremely rare. It does not apply at all to better than 99 percent of the abortions being done. Some doctors even say that modern knowledge and technology has made this cause for abortion nonexistent. And secondly, abortion for this reason was allowed in our country before the abortion revolution ever began. When abortion was recommended for this cause, it undoubtedly placed an agonizing decision upon the parents of the child, a decision over which we may be very reluctant to pass judgment, since one life was being weighed against another. In light of these considerations this rare but tragic case is totally irrelevant to the cause of permissive abortion.

A WOMAN HAS THE RIGHT OVER HER OWN BODY.

This seems to be the most common reason advanced for permissive abortion laws. It is essentially *the reason* cited in *Roe v. Wade.* But the court also acknowledged that this right of the woman which it called "privacy" is not absolute; it can, therefore, be overruled by other rights. When we recognize how empty this pro-abortion argument is, the complete bankruptcy of the abortionist's position will begin to manifest itself.

Pro-life groups would agree that a woman has a right over her own body; but is the unborn baby part of her body? Only someone who is totally ignorant of the facts would even suggest that such is the case. Is a tree part of the ground because its roots depend upon the ground for nutrition and support? Are you part of a car because you happen to be encased by the car at some moment? Even if we go along with the terrible analogy suggested by some abortionists and compare the baby to a parasite (ugh!), even a parasite is a separate and distinct organism. The blood streams of mother and child, and often the blood types, are separate and different, and in half of all cases the very sex of the infant is different from the mother.

The plain fact is that the unborn baby is a totally unique and separate human being. From the moment of conception he has his own genetic heritage and has a pre-programmed master-plan for growth and development. There is only one real interruption in this growth process and that is death; everything else unfolds in orderly sequence. All the unborn infant needs is nutrition and protection. His needs are essentially the same as those of any other human being.

Perhaps it is the right to privacy which is the point, however, and not a woman's right to her own body. (The whole argument is so ambiguous that it is difficult to know for sure what the pro-abortion argument actually is.) Does our right to privacy extend to the point of harming someone else? Does a father, for example, have the right to extend genuine harm to his children, even though that harm is done in the privacy of his own home? Obviously not. The fact that parents can be prosecuted for child-abuse demonstrates that our right to privacy does not include a right to harm others, not to mention actually killing them. So the argument really hinges on whether the unborn is a living human being as opposed to an unidentifiable glob of cells. As we have seen, medical knowledge quickly settles that question.

So this argument, perhaps the key point of the abortionists, is simply devoid of substance. It is strictly a hazy, emotional attempt to short-circuit proper rational and moral thought.

Yet women's rights are among the powerful political forces of today. Consequently it may be unpopular to oppose a practice so clouded by the feminist revolt as is abortion. The feminist movement is one of the very real political reasons for the abortion revolution. Many feminists have stated that they have two top political goals — ratification of the Equal Rights Amendment and abortion on demand. (There are also pro-life feminists, however.) What the pro-abortion feminists choose to ignore is that no one is forcing them to become pregnant. Therefore, no woman need have children if she does not wish to. But once conception has occurred, then no amount of equal rights gives a woman or doctor the right to kill another human being.

THE MENTAL OR PHYSICAL HEALTH OF THE MOTHER REQUIRES ABORTION.

This argument rests on the assumption that pregnancy is often damaging in some way to women, as opposed to abortion which is supposedly safe. It would be very difficult to demonstrate that such is the case. On the one hand, pregnancy and childbirth offer minimal risks for a woman today. In comparison to the benefits of childbirth (assuming children are a blessing to parents and the nation), the problems associated with pregnancy are a relatively minor factor.

On the other hand, the American public seems generally oblivious to the risks involved with abortion. Three British gynecologists describe several of these risks as follows:

> If the termination of pregnancy were as safe as so many advocates of liberal abortion maintain, a patient suffering as a result of the operation could claim that professional negligence was responsible for her subsequent distress or disaster. Such claims would be grossly unfair. There would be great sympathy for a 16 year old girl whose uterus was torn beyond repair; for the married woman with gut resection and peritonitis; for the mother in monthly distress following hysterotomy because of implantation endometritis in her abdominal wall, vagina or bladder; for the anxious infertile wife who knows the tubal damage now denies her the baby she desires is the delayed price she is paying for her teenage abortion. But the fact remains that none of these situations may be the result of negligence. They

are complications which, though well known to, and well documented by, those with wide experience of an operation which is neither simple or safe, are seldom mentioned by those who claim that abortion is safe and merely an extension of contraceptive techniques.[26]

Even Bella Abzug, one of our nation's prominent feminists, admits that the rate of serious complication for first trimester abortions is six per cent, and for second trimester abortions is from twenty to twenty-five per cent.[27]

One of our nation's leading physicians, Dr. C. Everett Koop, also speaks out about the complications from abortion. Says Koop:

> Unfortunately, the excellent records of the first five years of liberalized abortion under the National Health Service in Great Britain have revealed an increase in incidence of the following: illegitimacy, venereal disease, prostitution, later sterility of the previously aborted mother, pelvic inflammatory disease from gonorrhea, and subsequent spontaneous abortions or miscarriages. Ectopic pregnancies — that is, where the egg is fertilized not in the uterus but up in the fallopian tube, requiring an emergency abdominal operation — have doubled since abortion has been liberalized. Prematurity in women who have had a previous abortion has increased in Great Britian by 40 per cent.[28]

We should also keep in mind the steady rise in the frequency of abortion in our country. As the number of abortions increases, the complications resulting from abortion are bound to rise as well. It is very possible that the net effect of permissive abortion will mean more damage to the women involved than would have been the case under our former laws. But we are straying too far from the main issue here, because even if it were to the woman's medical advantage to have an abortion, this still does not begin to justify the killing of innocent persons.

A word should also be said about the matter of the woman's "mental health." It is very difficult to deal with this issue objectively, because there are no satisfactory means for determining if abortion does more good or more damage to a woman's mental health. Suffice it to say, if abortion benefits the mental health of any segment of the women involved with abortion, then such a thesis remains to be demonstrated. The opposite thesis may well be the case.

ABORTION IS REQUIRED TO ELIMINATE DEFECTIVES.

The first thing we should recognize about this argument is that these "defectives" the abortionist is talking about are really defective people. This issue, therefore, clarifies several of the ethical premises behind the abortion revolution. Does our right to life depend upon a certain level of I.Q.? Many of the defectives the abortionists would eliminate are the mentally retarded, such as mongoloid children. Or does our right to live depend upon the amount of contribution we can make to society? Ultimately we are forced to face the question: are we willing to protect and support those who cannot support themselves? Or will we direct all of our affluence towards our own satisfaction? The real question is — do people have an intrinsic right to live? Or do we have a right to live only if we can lead "meaningful" and/or productive lives?

The goal of having superior people, free from defectives, is called eugenics (good race). The fact that this was an essential goal of Hitler's mad utopia should make us at least a trifle suspicious. As Hitler demonstrated, the only way of eliminating defective people is by eliminating defective people. Is this really what our nation wants?

And who would be empowered to decide which baby should live and which should die? Should physicians have that right? Or the parents? Or the state? Is it not, perhaps, playing God to make that kind of decision? We shall see a bit later that playing God is precisely what many abortionists have in mind.

A frequent target of eugenic abortions is the child whose mother had German measles early in pregnancy. Most such children, however, are born perfectly normal. Should these normal infants be sacrificed in order to also eliminate the handicapped? And what of those who are born handicapped? Does deafness or blindness give a person less of a right to live than you or I enjoy? What kind of future would someone with the handicaps of Helen Keller have enjoyed under the philosophy of eugenics? Eugenic "mercy killings" are already being done to handicapped infants after they have been born. Such infanticide is the next logical step for the abortion revolution to take. How ironic it is that in this day of equal rights for the handicapped, the new-born and unborn handicapped are being denied the very right to live!

WOMEN WILL HAVE ABORTIONS ANYWAY: IT IS BETTER TO HAVE THEM UNDER SAFE AND LEGAL CONDITIONS.

We have already seen that legalization does not necessarily make abortions any safer, and that no abortion is really safe. But is it true that women will have abortions regardless of the legality? The experience of Romania should answer this question for us. By 1965, after many years of permissive abortion, Romania's birth rate had dropped to 14 births per thousand population.[29] Troubled by this clearly undesirable birth rate (ours now is about the same), the Romanian government sharply restricted abortion. The dramatic result was that the birth rate doubled the very next year! It simply is not true that women will get abortions regardless of the law. Some women will, but most will not.

Another example is that of the Soviet Union, the country with the longest experience with permissive abortion laws. The Soviet Union has allowed abortion off and on since 1920. As of 1965 the Soviet women were having an average of 2.3 children. And how many abortions do you suppose they were having? An average of six! In 1965 the Soviet Union had 10,600,000 legal abortions. If you compare that rate to the number of abortions in the United States, even if you include a high estimate of illegal abortions in the U.S., this would mean that we had only 3 percent as many abortions as the Soviet Union in that year.[30] There simply can be no doubt that permissive abortion laws greatly increase the number of abortions. The statement that most women will have abortions regardless of the law is directly contrary to the facts. We have already seen what the abortion revolution has done to our own birth rate and frequency of abortion.

Because the abortionists use this above argument so frequently, let us consider the example of one more country. The following description of abortion in Japan was included in the *Medical World News* of November 9, 1973:

ABORTION IN JAPAN AFTER 25 YEARS

Rising literally from the ashes of World War II, Japan has produced the economic miracle of the 20th century. To help make that miracle possible in its hungry, overcrowded islands, the Diet passed a liberal abortion law in 1948 as a means of holding the population down.

But on the 25th anniversary of that law, a saddened Japanese physician told colleagues from nearly 50 nations that his country's abortion policy has had some unfortunate consequences: Abortion is replacing contraception, and Japan has too few young people to care for the growing proportion of its population over 65.

"Abortion has become a way of life," Prof. T. S. Ueno of Tokyo's Nihon University told the Ninth Congress of the International Academy of Legal and Social Medicine in Rome. "Moral life has become disorderly. It is an age of free sex, and the life of the unborn is not respected. We can now say the law is a bad one."

Japanese physicians, Dr. Ueno said, can receive a "designation" to perform abortions after a two-year "apprenticeship." A doctor having this designation may operate if in his judgment "the mother's health may be affected seriously by continuation of pregnancy or delivery, from the physical or economic viewpoint."

A year after the "Eugenic Protection Law" was passed, 250,000 legal abortions were done, Dr. Ueno reports; last year no fewer than 1.5 million were done.

"Abortion has become a substitute for contraception," he says. "About half the Japanese women who have abortions admit that they did not even try to prevent conception. Induced abortion has become so common it is almost compulsory for women; they feel it is part of life in Japan that can't be helped. Some apartment house managers enforce a policy that no family in the building may have more than two children. Pregnant mothers are often asked by their gynecologists whether or not they intend to carry the child to term. The entire economy has hardened around the two-child family."

Many Japanese are ashamed of having abortions, he suggested. Public opinion surveys suggest that most Japanese women do not approve of abortion even though they practice it. Only 18% of women surveyed said that they "did not feel anything in particular" after their first abortion, 35% "felt sorry about the unborn child," and 28% felt they had "done something wrong," Dr. Ueno told the congress.

"Induced abortions are a source of easy income for doctors," he charged. "Cash is paid, so they don't have to be paid through health insurance; many find abortion to be a convenient source of side income."

He also charged that legal abortions are "not remarkably safer" than illegal ones. He believes the sudden change from pregnancy causes an imbalance of the sympathetic nervous system and has many other ill effects. Among them: dysmenorrhea, sterility, habitual spontaneous abortion, extrauterine pregnancies, cramps, headache, vertigo, exhaustion, sleeplessness, lumbago, neuralgia, debility and psychosomatic illness, perforation of the uterus, cervical lesions, infections, bleeding and retention of some tissue.

Another consequence of 25 years of abortion, according to Dr. Ueno: Japan has 14 million people over 65 among its population of 108 million. In the next 20 years the over-65 population is expected to reach 29 million, of a total of 130 million Japanese. Because this means too many old people for the young to support, he predicts strong pressure for euthanasia.

"Easy abortion has been a bad experience for us," he told MWN. "It is now very difficult to control or to eradicate, despite growing criticism. It has become a way of life; the law might be changed but the practice cannot be controlled.

"The sooner Japan returns to a solid law which forbids the taking of the life of the unborn, the better for our nation. Just as we need guard rails, signal lights, and speed limits, so we need precise laws governing abortion. We need such laws to save us from our individual and collective weakness," he concluded.[31]

IT IS BETTER TO HAVE ABORTION THAN UNWANTED CHILDREN WHO WILL BE ABUSED BY THEIR PARENTS.

Perhaps we should ask some of these unwanted children if they would consent to being killed as a solution to their being abused. Additionally, if abortion did actually reduce child-abuse, then we should see a dramatic reduction of such abuse, since we now have

1.3 million abortions annually. Do we find such a decrease? No! On the contrary, we are instead experiencing an epidemic of child abuse. A recent issue of *Time* observed that the experts in the field all agree that there is a genuine and dramatic increase in child abuse. These experts now estimate, says *Time,* that there are at least 2 million cases per year.[32]

It is not difficult to understand the reason for this upsurge in child abuse. Hand in hand with the abortion revolution has come a marked decrease in the value and respect given to children. We do not destroy that which we value. If you can kill them before they are born, why respect them after they are born? We can compare the loss of the unborn's rights to a slave's loss of rights; was there any compelling reason for a slave owner not to beat his slaves? Or not to break up slave families? Or not to have sexual relations with his slaves? To deny the right to freedom is to deny most other rights. To deny the right to life is to deny all rights! (The Supreme Court at one time refused to recognize slaves as persons under the Constitution.)

A college student whom I counseled several years ago gave a forceful and pathetic commentary on the connection between abortion and child-abuse. She told of various ways she had been mistreated by her parents, but there was one way which seemed to stand out in her mind above all else — her mother had repeatedly told her, "Just remember, we didn't need to have you either." A younger child, and only other sibling, had been killed by abortion. That mother's cruel verbal club was a candid and true statement on the genuine relationship between child-abuse and abortion. I do not believe I have ever heard more devastating words than those.

We might also ask if killing a child by abortion might not constitute child-abuse.

What of the "unwanted child" resulting from rape or incest? In the first place, these children are not unwanted; if the mother does not want them, there are any number of parents who do, and would give almost anything to adopt them. I am told that black-market babies now bring as high as $35,000. And since the abortion revolution many adoption agencies have closed their doors for lack of babies. Secondly, pregnancy resulting from either rape or incest is rare. National policies ought not be based on exceptional cases. And thirdly, the baby in the case of rape or incest is a totally innocent victim of the evil act. What kind of ethical system would kill the innocent victim in response to the crime of someone else?

About a year ago I counseled a college coed who said she had been raped. Even though pregnancy is extremely rare in such circumstances, she assured me that she was one of those rare cases. She had gone to see one of my colleagues earlier in the day; he had referred her to me upon learning she had an appointment with an abortion clinic for the next morning. I never told her directly not to go through with the abortion, but I did share with her some of the factual details about the nature of the life within her. I also asked her if she could justify taking the innocent infant's life when he too was a victim of the rape. She has since given birth to the baby, and somewhere in Southern Minnesota there lives a family with a newly adopted son or daughter, a child they never would have known if the abortionist had seen the mother first. Doesn't this make a lot more sense than abortion, even in the tough case of rape?

Three months before this baby was born I had spoken with another young woman, also a college student, who had been pregnant against her wishes. She had not been raped, however, but had simply gone along with her boy friend's demands. She told her story in tears, because she had had an abortion seven months earlier. In my counseling I have spoken with hundreds of troubled people, but I have never encountered someone as brokenhearted as she was. This woman knew she had taken her own baby's life and there was nothing anyone could do to bring that precious life back. You tell me — which of these two women made the right choice?

ABORTION IS NEEDED FOR POPULATION CONTROL.

There is no doubt that abortion reduces the population, at least over a short time span; but war, disease and starvation also reduce the population and we do not find many advocates of these other plagues. Of course abortion is a safer device for population reduction because it is always someone else who is being killed. Population reduction, however, is not the same thing as population control. In order to see the impact of permissive abortion on the population of the U.S., we can add the zero population growth rate to our former chart. (Zero Population growth rate is here defined as the level of reproduction where the number of reproducing daughters born to a woman of reproductive age is equal to one.) The result is as follows:[33]

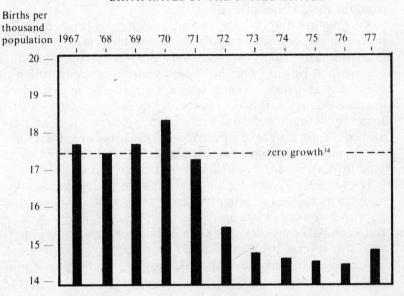

BIRTH RATES OF THE UNITED STATES

Several observations can be made from these statistics. In the first place, we can see that the United States had come very close to zero population growth without legalized abortion. We had actually reached zero growth in 1968 and then the birth rate began a moderate upswing. It is highly desirable for us to maintain some population increase in order to remain a strong nation.

In comparison to the U.S., Czechoslovakia, which has had permissive abortion since 1957, has begun to provide economic incentives for live births. The Czechoslovakian government gives a mother $250 for the birth of any child after the first, and then subsidizes the child at a rate of $60 per month for the first two years.[35] And what is Czechoslovakia's birth rate? It is 20 per thousand (1977), about the same as our rate before the abortion revolution and substantially higher than our present rate. The *Medical World News* reported that Czechoslovakia is trying to encourage births because its population has stagnated at 14,000,000, and as a result the economy has stagnated as well. Other effects of permissive abortion are also evident in Czechoslovakia, as premature births have risen by 50 percent and only one woman in ten now uses contraceptives of any kind.[36] Oh, if we could learn from the mistakes of others!

Keeping in mind that the abortion revolution began in 1970, the impact of permissive abortion on our birth rate is obvious from the graph. Does this mean that abortion has controlled our population? Hardly! Our birth rate was under control before permissive abortion. It is now out of control by being well below the desirable level. It is obvious that population control can be achieved without permissive abortion, since we had accomplished it before the revolution began. Legal abortion, therefore, is not only unnecessary for population control, in our case it actually destroyed the population control we had enjoyed.

The reader may wonder why, then, our total population continues to increase? The primary reason is that we have at present a disproportionately large number of persons of reproductive age and a comparatively small number of elderly people. This imbalance will reverse itself in 20 to 30 years, however. Unless our women begin having substantially more children, the population could be in a serious decline at that time.

What impact would a declining population have on our national defense? On our agricultural surpluses? Or on our economy as a whole? Who will pay the social security bills when the retirement age group is much larger and the number of wage earners is smaller? Social security has repeated shortfalls now; there is good reason to doubt that it can remain solvent 30 years from now. Let us also keep in mind that real income is now declining in the U.S. As the number of elderly becomes a greater economic burden, there will be increased pressure for the elimination of the more costly aged via euthanasia. This will simply be the next logical step for the abortion revolution, which places no particular value on human life. The criterion of "meaningful life" applies equally well to both ends of the life continuum.

WOMEN HAVE THE RIGHT TO CHOOSE WHETHER THEY WILL HAVE AN ABORTION.

We now arrive at what is becoming the primary argument in favor of legalized abortion. Regardless of anything else which can be said, the abortion advocates contend, it is the woman herself who must have the right to make the decision. Coinciding with this rationale, abortion proponents generally prefer to be called "pro-choice" rather than "pro-abortion," even though this terminology is an implied admission that abortion is evil. Many abortion backers will even go so far as to say that they do not actually favor abortion, but that they do favor, instead, the woman's right to make that decision for herself.

On the surface this argument sounds good, since none of us care to oppose the rights of others. But do women have the right to abortion? The answer to this question must be, no! In the first place, the Hippocratic Oath, which has been western civilization's accepted code of medical ethics for some 2,000 years, expressly forbids abortion. Secondly, the Constitution of the United States, which has been a world-model for the respect of basic human rights, knows nothing of a right to choose abortion. And thirdly, it is impossible that there could be a right to choose abortion, because a woman's rights could never override the infant's right to live, since the right to live is guaranteed by both the Declaration of Independence and the Constitution, and since equal protection for all is one of the most basic principles for a free nation. Hopefully, all of us will vigorously defend the basic human rights, but there simply is no such thing as a right to choose abortion.

We can conclude, therefore, that this last pro-abortion argument is very easy to dismiss. The contention is so weak that it is difficult to take seriously. But such being the case, why are the abortionists now making it their primary line of defense? This is a puzzling turn of events, is it not? The explanation is that there is a deeper, more fundamental revolution taking place in addition to the abortion revolution. Indeed, permissive abortion would never have occurred in our country without this other revolution preceeding it.

Because this other revolution is so important, the next chapter will be devoted to it.

CHAPTER 8

THE REAL REASON
FOR ABORTION

It does not take much study to see that permissive abortion laws could never be justified on the basis of the previous lines of argument. The basic rationale for the abortion revolution must lie deeper. This more fundamental reason, however, is not difficult to ascertain. We can begin to uncover it by means of a statement by Archibald Cox, first chief prosecutor for the Watergate investigations, who said:

> The opinion [Roe v. Wade] fails even to consider what I would suppose to be the most compelling interest of the State in prohibiting abortion: the interest in maintaining that respect for the paramount sanctity of human life which has always been at the center of western civilization . . . .[37]

Cox here reveals the only way that permissive abortion laws make sense. You cannot respect human life (which has been one of the most basic values of western government) and allow abortion on demand. For the abortion revolution to have occurred, therefore, there must have been a preceding denial of human life as an unconditional value. The Communist countries have never objected on moral grounds to abortion, because they give no particular value to human life. Neither have they any particular regard for other basic human rights, of course. Permissive abortion laws and lack of respect for human life must go together. Since the right to life is the most basic of all rights, the abortion advocates should recognize that ultimately their ethical system denies that there are any fundamental human rights whatsoever. But perhaps many abortion proponents have not cared to explore their system of thought to its unpleasant conclusions.

Do you think that too much is being made of the Cox statement? Consider then the testimony of John McCollister:

The crux of the whole controversy centers around what moral value this life [unborn baby's] possesses and to what extent the law of our country should extend protection to that life. American law gave the benefit of every doubt to the existence and continuation of the unborn child's life. The Supreme Court decision has turned the law upside down. The rights of these unborn children are now being ignored.[38]

We will return a bit later to what it means to have "turned the law upside down." Consider also the statement of Senator James Buckley:

Given the indisputable reality of the fact that abortion involves the taking of a distinct human life, this places the focus on what is basically at issue: Will American society accept a new ethic that reduces human life from a supreme value to be granted full Constitutional protection from the moment of conception until death, or will it be downgraded to one of a number of values to be weighed in determining whether a particular life shall be terminated? This is something that the most honest advocates of permissive abortion have always understood.[39]

Buckley and McCollister make it very clear — hand-in-hand with the abortion revolution has come a new system of ethics which places no particular value on human life. We previously quoted from an editorial in *California Medicine* (page 37), describing this same revolution in ethics. Let us now consider another part of that editorial:

The process of eroding the old ethic and substituting the new has already begun. It may be most clearly seen in changing attitudes toward human abortion. In defiance of the long held Western ethic of intrinsic and equal value for every human life regardless of its stage, condition, or status, abortion is becoming accepted by society as moral, right, and even necessary.[40]

The previous four quotations — the last being from a pro-abortion writer — all agree that a totally new system of morality is behind the abortion revolution. Just what is this new ethic which is replacing the old one? The new morality in government is well described by Senator Mark Hatfield of Oregon:

I have wrestled with my beliefs about abortion — morally, legally, biologically, sociologically, and theologically. In doing so, convictions that I find totally compelling have been deeply affirmed. Moreover, I am persuaded that how society regards this question directly relates to whether we can choose to nourish and enhance all life for the development of its full humanity, or whether we shall make quiet compromises about the sacredness of human life, until the fundamental worth of any life becomes subject to society's discretion, rather than guaranteed by that life's being.[41]

Here we have a brief, but concise, statement on the new ethics. This new system asserts that the norm for moral judgments is "society's discretion" and that any and all other moral values, such as the right to life, will have to yield before the whims of society. All intrinsic human rights and moral values are being dethroned and replaced by society's discretion.

Seen in this way, the abortion revolution makes sense. The pro-abortion forces, who are now largely in control in the United States, place a higher value on the pregnant woman's "right" to decide for herself than they place on the life of the child. It is that simple. If the baby might be retarded, or if the health of the mother is in question, it is just that much easier for the abortionists to rationalize their decision. That the woman or the physician have no right to murder another human being makes no difference under this kind of moral reasoning; if society (the abortion society) says the woman has the right, then she has the right.

Under this new system of ethics there are no universal standards for determining right and wrong. Whatever society values will be protected; whatever society fails to value will be destroyed. Since society's values are subject to change, no one will ever have the assurance of the protection of his own rights. According to this new system there are no intrinsic or absolute rights; we are all at the mercy of society's judgments. The opinion polls theoretically become the sacred writings of this new ethic, because the measuring of popular opinion becomes the way of determining right and wrong.

This is how the law has been turned upside down. Our country was founded on the principle that all people have certain intrinsic rights. These rights are not given by society. Indeed they exist whether society recognizes them or not. These rights are ours by virtue of our creation as human beings. The founding fathers of our nation had a clear understanding of these intrinsic rights, therefore, they insisted in the Declaration of Independence that the rights were "unalienable," that is, they cannot be removed from us. This Declaration of Independence makes it very clear that our rights are not granted us by society or government. On the contrary, the Declaration asserts that the rights reside within us and must, therefore, be recognized and protected by government. The Declaration also insists that any government which does injury to these rights has lost its right to govern, and may be altered or even overthrown by the people. Our Constitution builds on this same understanding which is laid down in the Declaration, and for that reason this Constitution includes the Bill of Rights to ensure that our basic intrinsic rights would be protected by the government. Such a guarantee of our basic rights was seen as a necessary element of good government — our rights were to come first, and just government was to rest upon and protect these inherent rights of the individuals governed.

In direct contrast to the ethical system of our forefathers, the new moral system stipulates that there are no universal or intrinsic rights. It is then up to society to decide what rights people should have. Since, in practice, it is the government that either protects rights or fails to do so, in effect it becomes the government's power to decide what our rights are.

The following diagram will illustrate the difference between the new ethic and the former ethic:

Government rests on the _____ unalienable human rights:	This is the ethical premise which is the basis of our democracy, as clearly stated by our nation's fundamental documents.
All human rights rest _____ on governmental policies:	This is the new ethic. Persons have only those rights granted them by society; in practice, persons have whatever rights government chooses to grant.

This is what it means to have turned the law upside down.

An extension of this new ethic is the quality of life ethic. If we assume that society decides what is of value and what is not, then society has the power to dictate that the quality of life is more important than having life. This is exactly what many social innovators have done. They argue that since a mongoloid child, for example, has a low quality of life, or that a family's quality of life is decreased by having such a child, or that society's quality of life is threatened by having to care for such children, then the "right" thing to do is to eliminate such children via abortion or infanticide. Viewed in this fashion, the killing of such a child is seen as an act of love. Again we see the law turned upside down.

Another extension of the new ethic is utilitarianism. Assuming that society decides what is right and what is wrong, then society can choose utilitarianism. This is a system of ethics which stipulates that an action is judged right or wrong only in terms of the end result of that action, no actions are right or wrong in themselves. Let us keep in mind that society would be the judge of what results are good and what results are bad. If, therefore, a nation's quality of life is judged to be improved by the killing of 1.3 million infants through abortion each year, then the utilitarian ethicist concludes that such killing is not only permissible, but that it is a positive moral good. Hitler concluded that the end goal of achieving a superior German society justified the killing of millions of Jews. Again, this is what it means to have our system of law turned upside down.

There are several disturbing aspects of this new ethic. Not the least of these is the fact that utilitarianism is the ethical philosophy of Communism. This is why we now have essentially the same abortion policy as the Soviet Union and other Communist countries. A second very practical concern is the question of who will decide what policies are morally right. Agreement with our Constitution ceases to be a vital concern, since a utilitarian would have no qualms about violating the Constitution if he feels the end result is right. Moreover, the will of the majority ceases to be an adequate check on governmental policies, because the utilitarian can justify violating majority rule if he feels the end effect justifies it. So even though the opinion polls are theoretically the norm for the new ethic, in actuality the only norm becomes the decisions of government. There ceases to be any check on governmental actions, because anything can be rationalized as being to the ultimate good of the country. It is not by coincidence that utilitarianism and authoritarianism walk hand in hand.

As a matter of fact, there is good evidence that the abortion revolution conflicts with the majority rule principle. According to the Gallup Poll, as described by the *Minneapolis Tribune* of April 22, 1979, a majority of Americans would allow abortion only if the mother's life is endangered, or during the first trimester in the case of pregnancy resulting from rape or incest. In all other cases the majority of Americans would not allow abortion. Even though the American majority is not quite as protective of the unborn's right to life as should be the case, nevertheless, this same majority is far more protective than the present law under *Roe* and *Doe.* The American majority is even more protective of the right to life than the laws of the states which, in the late 1960s, went along with recommendations of the American Medical Association. The permissive abortion produced by *Roe v. Wade,* then, is inconsistent with the majority's values. (The results of this Gallup Poll are included in Appendix A.)

When the abortion advocates focused on the Supreme Court, they successfully bypassed the wishes of much of the public. Since the justices never face the voting public, we who follow the pro-life philosophy have no adequate check on them even though we may be in the majority. So beware of the abortionist's claims that the majority of Americans share their views.* This is quite probably not true. Those who place no value on an infant's right to life are perfectly willing to distort opinion polls in order to attempt to justify their actions. These abortion advocates intend to shape public values, not follow them.

Because the Supreme Court has disregarded American opinion and acted contrary to the Constitution's clear right to life principle, the pro-life groups have been attempting to enact a human life amendment to the Constitution. This would force the Court to recognize basic Constitutional principles as well as the will of the majority. Whether this effort will be successful remains to be seen.

Meanwhile, in the case of permissive abortion we have an undeniably dictatorial rule by the few. This kind of authoritari-

---

* Editor's note: There are conflicting statistics as to just where the American public stands in regard to abortion. This of course only underscores the author's warnings concerning any system of ethics based on majority opinion.

anism must be the final result of the new ethical system. Even though this new ethic always speaks of human rights, it has no other choice but to make government the final authority.

It is theoretically and practically impossible that a democracy can survive the new ethic. One or the other must be destroyed. In a democracy there must be some absolute guarantee of our intrinsic rights. The new ethic cannot even assert that absolute rights exist, let alone make any guarantees.

HUMANISM VERSUS NATURAL
LAW

As we would expect, the new ethic has not arisen independently. Ethics are always but a part of a larger philosophy of life. In the United States the ideology which is primarily responsible for promoting the new ethic is humanism. Or, more precisely, the new ethic is part of the humanistic world-view.

What is humanism? Perhaps we should go to humanism's own definition of itself in order to understand what the basic humanistic beliefs are. The Humanist Manifesto II is the latest creed of humanism and this statement makes the humanistic position quite clear. The Manifesto explains that humanism is a rather broad philosophy, encompassing Marxism (Communist ideology), atheism, agnosticism, skepticism and liberal religion. The most basic core belief of humanism is the rejection of God's existence. The Manifesto states: "*We find insufficient evidence for belief in the existence of a supernatural*" (Manifesto's emphasis). In place of God, humanism asserts that man is the highest form of life (hence the name "humanism"), as stated by the Manifesto: "We begin with humans not God. . . ." We can see, therefore, that the essence of humanism is placing man in the stead of God; or, we might say, humanism is the view that man is god.

Humanism even has its own messiah. The Manifesto states: "*No deity will save us; we must save ourselves*" (Manifesto's emphasis). And how will humanism accomplish its mission of saving mankind? It will do so, states the Manifesto, by "radically new human purposes and goals." In other words, the humanists intend to chart an entirely new (radically new) type of civilization for our nation (and the entire world) in order to promote their brand of utopia.

Humanistic morality follows logically from its basic ideology. In the humanist's view there is no God, only nature. In nature there is ultimately no right or wrong in a moral sense. It is not wrong for rivers to flood, nor is it right for rivers to stay within their banks. Neither is it wrong for a monkey to abandon its young. We humans might not like such an act, but monkeys are totally free from any kind of ethics. In nature things just are; they are not right or wrong. If people are simply part of nature rather than being creations of God, then it follows that no human acts are either right or wrong. It cannot then be wrong to engage in homosexual acts, or to dissolve marriages, or to kill infants by abortion. The best a humanist can do is to assert total human freedom and individuality, and then suggest that something is "right or wrong for you." Governmental laws to the humanist become a collective agreement (social contract) whereby individuals agree on common ethical principles for their collective community. And as we have seen, the norm for these standards can only be "society's discretions," even though the real norm turns out to be, in effect, the decisions of the government.

The Humanist Manifesto II very clearly embraces the system of ethics as stated above. The Manifesto declares: "We affirm that moral values derive their source from human experience. Ethics is autonomous and situational, needing no religious or ideological sanction." Actually this position is self-contradictory, since humanism is the ideological sanction behind humanistic ethics.

To be consistent the humanists should say that a country's abortion policy should be whatever that country would collectively agree on. But apparently the humanists give priority to unrestrained individual freedom as opposed to majority rule. The Manifesto states: "The right to abortion . . ." is one of our basic rights, as well as the right to divorce, suicide, euthanasia and homosexual practice. The Manifesto makes no mention of the right to life, obviously, as that would directly contradict the right to abortion.

The contrast between the Humanist Manifesto and the Declaration of Independence is striking. The Declaration insists that our rights are given us by our Creator, and that these rights include the right to life, liberty and the pursuit of happiness. In contrast, the Manifesto insists that our rights are given us by man, and that these rights include the right to abortion, divorce and homosexual acts. The Humanists were not exaggerating when they said that their utopia demanded "radically new" purposes and goals. This humanist ideology is nothing less than a revolt from the basic principles of our free nation.

And how will humanism promote its noble ethical system? By means of, says the Manifesto, "Moral education for children and adults as an important way of developing awareness and sexual maturity." From this statement it is evident that humanists see sex education and values clarification as primary devices for advocating their ethical system. Psychologist Lawrence Kohlberg of Harvard has pointed out, however, that it is impossible to teach such things as sex education without also teaching a system of ethics. The only real question is which ethics will be taught.[42]

Since humanists place no particular value on human life, there is nothing to prevent the killing of persons through means other than abortion. For example, Dr. Joseph Fletcher, probably humanism's most influential ethical philosopher, reportedly advocates "quality control standards" which would eliminate those persons whose lives do not measure up to an acceptable adult level. Other humanists are contending that a baby should not be declared a person until three days after birth. That way the defectives missed by abortion could be eliminated without legal problems.[43] How much closer to Hiter's holocaust can we get?

It is all too obvious, therefore, that humanism actively promotes the killing of innocent persons, so long as their deaths are viewed as being consistent with the "quality of life" that humanists are seeking. Remember how C. S. Lewis described the forces of evil as being willing to sacrifice human lives when it was seen as being to their own advantage. Humanism is nothing other than the new form of the old evil powers. The new morality is nothing other than the old immorality. Permissive abortion is one of the surface results of unrestrained evil. This may sound too simple, but it is essentially the truth of the matter.

The net result of the humanistic ethic is by no means limited to the abortion revolution, however. Other evil results are well described by former Congresswoman Clare Boothe Luce in her speech: "Is the New Morality Destroying America?" Her answer to that speech title is an emphatic "yes." The new ethic has produced, argues Luce, increased divorce, incest, desertion by spouses, child abuse, alcoholism, rape, abortion, prostitution, drug addiction, homosexual practice, pornography, and the like.[44] Perhaps it is time that Americans take a hard look down the road that this country is now traveling and ask if this is really the "brave new world" that is desired. Humanism promises utopia. It delivers death and destruction.

If the reader has any doubts concerning the causal link between the rise in humanism and the abortion revolution, he should consider the political forces behind *Roe* and *Doe*. John T. Noonan has pointed out that the three political groups which have had the greatest influence on these court decisions are Planned Parenthood of America, the Civil Liberties Union and the National Organization of Women.[45] It is quite obvious that these three groups are advocates of humanist ideology — Alan Guttmacher, President of Planned Parenthood, and Betty Friedan, founder of the National Organization of Women, are both signers of the Humanist Manifesto II. The Civil Liberties Union has consistently championed humanistic causes and has just as consistently opposed the interests of Christian churches and schools.

In direct contrast to the ethics of humanism is the moral code of Christianity. Biblical Christian ethics insist that it is wrong to take an innocent person's life, that it is wrong to have sexual relations with your neighbor's wife, that it is wrong to divorce your spouse, that it is wrong to engage in homosexual relations, and the like. In other words, Christian ethics calls for the protection of the right to life for all human beings. It also calls for the protection of marriage, property, our good name, chastity and everything else that is of real value.

Christianity recognizes that there is genuine evil in this world, and that, therefore, all which is good must be protected from the ravages of evil deeds. Christian ethics in no way discourages or impedes personal fulfillment or enjoyment. On the contrary, Christian ethics provide the framework within which honest and beneficial endeavors can flourish and the common good of mankind can be advanced. If our nation would return to Christian ethical codes, the abortion revolution would come to an end and many of the other evils mentioned would be largely restrained as well.

But this understanding raises another question. Given the principle of the distinction between church and state, why should the government follow the ethical principles of one religion, in this case Christianity? Would that not be a mixing of church and state? On the surface it would seem so, but actually no improper mixing of church and state occurs when Christian ethics are followed by the state. The reason is that the ethics of Christianity are not unique to the Christian world-view. On the contrary, Christianity simply recognizes and teaches the universal moral codes which are common to all people. As is clearly stated in *Romans* chapters one and two, all people recognize intuitively that it is wrong to murder others, that it is wrong to break marriages, that it is wrong to engage in homosexuality, and the like. In other words, all people instinctively recognize the truth of the moral codes which are embraced by Christianity. Actually it is not quite accurate to speak of "Christian ethics," because Christianity has no corner on these moral values. Christianity only includes within itself the one true moral system which is the common property of all mankind.

Because these ethical values are instinctive in all men, the moral system is often called "natural law." It is natural because it is ours by nature. It is law because it is the one true moral law upon which all just governmental laws must rest. Excellent expressions of natural law include the Golden Rule (Do unto others as you would have them do unto you), the Ten Commandments, and the Biblical summary of the moral law ("Love the Lord your God with all your heart and with all your soul, and with all your strength," and "love your neighbor as yourself." Deuteronomy 6:5, Leviticus 19:18).

The reason our nation used to be such an outstanding example of the protection of human rights (with some exceptions, of course) was because this country was founded squarely on natural law. It was to natural law that the Declaration of Independence appealed to justify our separation from Great Britain. (It is natural law which is meant by the Declaration's words: "the laws of Nature and of Nature's God.") When the Declaration proceeded to describe the "unalienable rights" which are "self-evident" and are given us by our Creator, it was again speaking directly and clearly of natural law. The Constitution with its Bill of Rights was built on this natural law foundation which was laid down so unmistakably in the Declaration.

Oh, if our people only knew that our nation is founded on natural law! Perhaps then they would see that the unborn child's right to life cannot be denied in America. Perhaps then they would see that humanism with its new ethic is undermining the very foundation of our country.

But humanism has succeeded in removing natural law from our vocabulary. Many Americans, perhaps most, do not even know what the term "natural law" means. Instead we hear the humanistic phrases like, "Do your own thing," and "If it is right for you, then it is right," and "If it feels good, do it."

It is high time our nation rejected humanism and returned to the basic principles upon which this nation was built and because of which our country became great. Ultimately our freedom depends on it. Right now the lives of our unborn children depend on it. It is time that we speak of what our Declaration of Independence and Constitution really mean. It is time that we speak again of the unalienable rights which have been given us by our Creator, and upon which all just government rests. It is time that we again understand the reality of natural law and recognize that natural law is essential to democracy. Only then will the abortion revolution come to an end. Only then will the right to life again be an essential part of the law of our land.

CHAPTER 10

THE RIGHT TO LIFE

The pro-life argument is simple and it is this: According to the most basic principles upon which our country was founded, all people have a basic right to live. This right does not depend upon our being able to sustain ourselves independently, nor does it depend upon our having a certain level of I.Q., nor does it depend upon any other quality of life standard, nor does it depend upon our contribution to society, nor does it depend upon our living outside the womb, nor does it depend upon the values of society or laws of government at any particular time. The right to life is a God-given right of all human beings.

This right is not granted by the state; indeed, it cannot be granted by anyone. On the contrary, the right to life must be recognized and protected by the state. (The Jews who were murdered by the Nazis had just as much of a right to life as you and I enjoy.) All of the basic rights reside within each individual, and we delegate certain of these rights to the state for the purpose of good order. The right to life is the most basic of all rights, because if we can be deprived of our life, then we are effectively deprived of all other rights as well.

It cannot be denied that the unborn baby is a human being and that he is, therefore, a person in the full sense. Being a person does not depend upon some particular stage of development, nor does it depend upon being mentally aware at some particular time, nor does it depend upon our being conceived in a loving relationship, nor does it depend upon any other similar conditions. Being a person depends only upon being a living human being. (The first definition which *The American Heritage Dictionary of the English Language* gives for "person" is: "A living human being, especially as distinguished from an animal or thing." The other dictionaries agree that this is the plain and primary meaning of the word "person.")

It cannot be denied that the right to life for every human being is one of the most basic principles upon which this nation was founded. The second paragraph of the Declaration of Independence begins as follows:

> We hold these truths to be self-evident, that all men are created equal, that they are endowed by their Creator with certain unalienable rights, that among these are Life, Liberty, and the Pursuit of Happiness. That, to secure these rights, Governments are instituted among men, deriving their just powers from the consent of the governed. That, whenever any form of government becomes destructive of these ends, it is the Right of the People to alter or to abolish it . . .

We can clearly see that this Declaration insists that the right to life is absolute and that it is the first and foremost of all rights. The Declaration also insists that this right to life is God-given; it is to be recognized by the state, not granted by the state. The Declaration further states that the right to life, and all other rights, reside within the individual. The purpose of just government, says the Declaration, is to ensure that these basic rights are protected. The Constitution of the United States is based upon these noble principles so clearly laid down in the Declaration. The Declaration is the foundation; the Constitution is the structure — built with its Bill of Rights to guarantee the protection of the God-given rights, number one being life!

The right to life position does not depend upon any particular religious belief. On the contrary, the right to life depends upon the very moral principles which are fundamental to all religions and which are basic to all free peoples. Even though many people will try to deny or repress the right to life, they can never do so completely. They will quickly invoke the right to life as soon as their own life is at stake. (Just as thieves will never allow theft amongst themselves.)

The right to life philosophy also depends upon the factual, scientific data which clearly indicates that the unborn infant is a living human being from the moment of conception onward. It is not surprising that the majority opinion of *Roe v. Wade* chose to ignore this wealth of objective data. Neither is it surprising that the pro-abortion spokesmen typically ignore this same data. They do not care to speak of heart beats, brain waves, hands and feet, the forty-six chromosomes, and the continuity of life, because it is all too obvious that this unborn being is a human life.

The real debate is one of morality. Will our nation continue to abandon those moral principles which have made it great, or will our country reaffirm its just foundation of the natural law principles which are self-evident to all? Will our nation again extend its arm of protection to all people, or will it follow the humanist lead and speak of quality of life in place of life itself? The choice is nothing less than just and democratic government versus tyranny.

The right to life position recognizes the equal rights of the pregnant woman as compared to the rights of the child. It is not true that the right to life camp is unsympathetic to the needs and rights of the pregnant woman. But the right to life philosophy insists that our rights end at that point where the rights of another begin. None of us have the right to end the lives of innocent human beings. Nor do we have the right to harm others in any way. Only the state may be delegated the right to kill, and then only under threat of war or by due process of law in retribution for criminal acts.

ATTACKS ON THE RIGHT TO LIFE POSITION.

Since the pro-life position is grounded on the truth, there is no way of successfully attacking it. Nevertheless, pro-abortionists do succeed to some extent in confusing and distorting the pro-life assertions. Several of the common attacks are as follows:

(1) "Pro-life is really a religious position. Since our nation follows the separation of church and state, the pro-life principles are out of place in government." This attack is totally false. The right to life is, as we have seen, part of the instinctive knowledge of all mankind. As the Declaration stated, the right to life is self-evident. Even though many church bodies actively support the pro-life movement, they do so on the basis of natural law and out of love for their fellow man, not out of any particular religious doctrine peculiar to their denomination.

Abortionists have also attempted to label the pro-life position as a Roman Catholic belief, but actually the Roman Church is only one of many bodies which actively support the pro-life movement. The Lutheran Church — Missouri Synod, the Wisconsin Evangelical Lutheran Synod, and the Evangelical Lutheran Synod are among the other bodies which have declared a strong pro-life position.

Sad to say, many other church bodies have adopted a "pro-choice" stance, and still others have been afraid to say anything on the matter at all for fear of alienating some of their members. These latter groups are the liberal churches; they have become more humanistic than Biblical. Let us remember that the Humanist Manifesto includes liberal religion within its own camp, so the pro-abortion statements of the liberal churches ought not surprise us.

Actually this argument that pro-life is supposedly a religious position is self-contradictory. The distinction between church and state is just as much a religious position as is the right to life. It is not possible to invoke one against the other, because if the right to life is a religious doctrine, then the grounds for objecting, which is the distinction between church and state, is also a religious doctrine. In actuality, both principles are precepts of natural law, therefore neither one violates the other.

(2) "Abortion is a matter of private morality; no one has the right to force their personal moral views on others." This attack is also false, because abortion is not a matter of private morality. Equal protection for all under the law, and protection of innocent human lives are among the most basic precepts of government. Who can seriously contend that the killing of human beings is not the concern of the state? Only someone who believes in anarchy (the belief that there should be no government at all) could seriously advance this objection.

(3) "The religious bodies which object to abortion do so because of their religious doctrine of ensoulment." The idea of this argument is essentially the same as the first objection, since this is merely one way of saying that pro-life is a religious position. It is true that Biblical theology recognizes that the living soul exists at the moment of conception, and it is true that this theology reinforces the awareness of many that this is a human life which is being killed in abortion. Nevertheless, a Christian's opposition to permissive abortion does not *depend* on the Biblical teaching that a human soul exists at conception, because, as we have seen, the medical-scientific facts also demonstrate that human life begins at conception. The religious teaching that all human lives are

souls is beside the point. Christians realize that questions involving the soul are not the concern of the state, but that questions concerning human lives are properly the government's responsibility.

Separation of church and state, private versus public morality, and ensoulment are all false issues. None of them in any way weaken the right to life case. By these points the abortionists simply distort or confuse what pro-life groups are saying. There are only three major questions which are genuinely relevant to the abortion issue. These questions are: Is the unborn a living human being (person)? Does each person have an intrinsic right to life? And, do all persons deserve equal protection under the law?

Because there is no serious doubt that the answer to each of these questions is yes, all people should actively support pro-life. The right to life philosophy rests on the most basic premises of a free country together with the scientific fact that the unborn is a human life. If we follow the most basic universal moral precept of all just ethical systems, namely that we should treat others as we would have them treat us, then the only conclusion which can be drawn is that all persons, born or unborn, healthy or infirm, of high intelligence or low intelligence, very young or very old —that absolutely all persons have an intrinsic and unalienable right to life. To say otherwise is to deny the foundation of democracy, the foundation of all just government and the essence of right versus wrong.

CHAPTER 11

OUR TASK

As C. S. Lewis so brilliantly illustrated, the battle between good and evil will continue until the last trumpet sounds. Meanwhile the powers of evil will destroy many. But men of good will shall strive to do everything within their power to ensure that the vulnerable are protected. The pro-life groups are engaged in many educational and political activities, and, for many of them, the focal point of these efforts is the enactment of a human life amendment to the United States Constitution. It is recognized that such an amendment would add nothing new to the Constitution, but it would prevent the Supreme Court from violating the right to life principles already contained therein. Such an amendment would have the immediate effect of overturning the Court's rulings in *Roe* and *Doe*.

Many such amendments have been submitted to Congress. One of these, as submitted by Representative Oberstar of Minnesota, reads as follows:

> SECTION 1. With respect to the right to life, the word 'person' as used in this article and in the fifth and fourteenth Articles of Amendment to the Constitution of the United States applies to all human beings irrespective of age, health, function or condition of dependency, including their unborn offspring at every stage of their biological development.
>
> SECTION 2. No unborn person shall be deprived of life by any person: *Provided, however,* that nothing in this article shall prohibit a law permitting only those medical procedures required to prevent the death of the mother.
>
> SECTION 3. The Congress and the Several States shall have power to enforce this article by appropriate legislation.[46]

The Lutheran Church — Missouri Synod has just recently stated its support of a human life amendment.[47] May the rest of us also join hands in calling for the enactment of such an amendment, and may we earnestly work to accomplish whatever else is possible for the protection of our unborn citizens.

Christians have particular reason for supporting the pro-life cause. As Christians we know that God has first loved us and that we cannot help but share that love with the rest of his children. We know that out of his grace he sent his only Son, Jesus, to live and to die for us in order to bring us into his kingdom. We know that he has commissioned us to carry out his tasks of love: the proclaiming of this gospel to the entire world, and the sustaining of the needy in this same world. As members of his church our primary goal is the sharing of the gospel of Christ. As members of the state our primary goal is the protection of all who are in need. May God move us to increased efforts in the promotion of these two tasks. May he move our nation to again affirm the basic rights which he has given to all mankind, and may he raise up leaders who will again ensure that the right to life of our children is duly recognized as an essential part of the law of our land.

APPENDIX A.

The results of a Gallup Poll, as described by the *Minneapolis Tribune* of April 22, 1979, reveal the public's attitude toward permissive abortion. The outcome of this poll is as follows:

"Do you think abortions should be legal under any circumstances, legal under only certain circumstances or illegal in all circumstances?"

	1975	1977	1979
Legal under all circumstances	21%	22%	22%
Legal only under certain circumstances	54%	55%	54%
Illegal under all circumstances	22%	19%	19%
No opinion	3%	4%	5%

It is evident from these results that the majority would allow abortion only under certain conditions. To determine what those conditions are, the following question was asked those who had said abortion should be legal only under certain circumstances:

"Now, thinking about the first three months of pregnancy (the second three months, the third three months), under which of these circumstances (respondents were handed a card with six circumstances listed) do you think abortions should be legal?"

	First trimester	Second trimester	Third trimester
1. When the woman's life is endangered	78%	66%	59%
2. When the woman's mental health is endangered	59%	32%	19%

81

3. When the pregnancy
   is a result of rape or
   incest   53%   46%   33%
4. When there is a chance
   the baby will be
   deformed   44%   37%   28%
5. When the woman may
   suffer severe physical
   health damage   42%   31%   22%
6. If the family cannot af-
   ford to have the child   15%   6%   4%

APPENDIX B.

POSITION STATEMENT OF THE EVANGELICAL
LUTHERAN SYNOD ON ABORTION

WHEREAS, All people are commanded by God to love their neighbor as they love themselves, and

WHEREAS, The Scriptures teach that human life begins at conception (Matthew 1:20, Psalm 51:5, Psalm 139:13-15), and

WHEREAS, Each Christian must recognize that abortion is the taking of a human life and is therefore a grievous sin except in the rare instance of it being used to save a mother's life, therefore,

A. BE IT RESOLVED, That we ask each congregation of our Synod to study this issue, and

B. BE IT FURTHER RESOLVED, That our Evangelical Lutheran Synod encourage its congregational members to confess publicly that the unborn child is a living person whose right to live must be protected.

This statement was adopted by the synod convention of June 1978.

APPENDIX C.

POSITION STATEMENT OF THE WISCONSIN
EVANGELICAL LUTHERAN SYNOD
ON ABORTION

WHEREAS

1) The Holy Scriptures clearly teach that the living yet unborn are persons in the sight of God and are under the protection of His Commandment against murder (Job 10:9-11; Ex. 20:13; Ps. 139:13; Matt. 5:21; Gen. 9:6; Jer. 1:5; Ps. 51:5; Luke 1:41-44); and

WHEREAS

2) our hearts are grieved over the millions of unborn who are being murdered each year through the sin of willful abortion; and

WHEREAS

3) our Synod has historically testified against abortion; except when it is medically necessary to save the life of the mother; therefore be it

RESOLVED,

a) That we encourage our Synodical periodicals as well as our pastors and teachers to continue fervently and faithfully to testify against abortion; and be it further

RESOLVED,

b) That we continue to urge our membership to make God's will in this matter known to our fellowmen whenever the opportunity presents itself; and be it further

RESOLVED,   c) That we encourage our membership to express their concern and compassion for distressed pregnant women by supporting the development of alternative to abortion programs which are consistent with God's Word; and be it finally

RESOLVED,   d) That we more zealously preach the Gospel of Christ which alone can change the wicked hearts of men and turn them from sin to righteousness.

This statement was adopted in August, 1979. The *Milwaukee Journal,* August 4, 1979 said of this statement:

The Wisconsin Evangelical Lutheran Synod, in an unprecedented action, voted overwhelmingly Friday to oppose abortion.

Traditionally, the theologically conservative synod has refrained from taking positions on social issues, and most of the debate on the abortion statement centered on that change in tradition and not on the substance of the resolution itself.

The Rev. Richard F. Weber of Lake Geneva, who submitted the resolution on behalf of a floor committee to the 425 delegates, said it was necessary to do so because "abortion is an outrageous, flagrant, revolting violation of God's holy will."

APPENDIX D.

POSITION STATEMENT OF THE LUTHERAN CHURCH — MISSOURI SYNOD ON ABORTION

WHEREAS, The Lutheran Church — Missouri Synod throughout its history has opposed abortion and since 1971 has spoken in convention to condemn "willful abortion as contrary to the will of God"; and

WHEREAS, We as members of Christian congregations have the obligation to protest this heinous crime against the will of God legally sanctioned in the United States and other lands; and

WHEREAS, The practice of abortion, its promotion, and legal acceptance are destructive of the moral consciousness and character of the people of any nation; therefore be it

Resolved, That the Lutheran Church — Missouri Synod in convention urgently call upon Christians

1. To hold firmly to the clear Biblical truths that, (a) the living but unborn are persons in the sight of God from the time of conception (Job 10:9-11; Ps. 51:5; 139:13-17; Jer. 1:5; Luke 1:41-44); (b) as persons the unborn stand under the full protection of God's prohibition against murder (Gen. 9:6; Ex. 20:13; Num. 35:33; Acts 7:19; 1 John 3:15); and (c) since abortion takes a human life, abortion is not a moral option, except as a tragically unavoidable by-product of medical procedures necessary to prevent the death of another human being, viz., the mother; and

2. To speak and act as responsible citizens on behalf of the living but unborn in the civic and political arena to secure for these defenseless persons due protection under the law; and

3. To offer as an alternative to abortion supportive understanding, compassion and help to the expectant parent(s) and

family, and to foster concern for unwanted babies, encouraging Lutheran agencies and families to open their hearts and homes to their need for life in a family; and be it further

Resolved, That the Synod earnestly encourage its pastors, teachers, officers, and boards

1. To warn publicly and privately (Prov. 31:8-9) against the sin of abortion;

2. To instruct the community of God that abortion is not in the realm of Christian liberty, private choice, personal opinion, or political preference;

3. To nurture a deep reverence and gratitude for God's gracious gift of human life;

4. To oppose in a responsible way attitudes and policies in congregations, schools, hospitals, Lutheran Social Service agencies, and other institutions within their sphere of influence and work which suggest that abortion is a matter of personal choice;

5. To support the efforts of responsible pro-life groups in their communities, e.g., "Lutherans for Life" (CTCR Report, CW, p. 74); and

6. To promote clear instruction of Christian morality in homes, schools, and churches of the Synod, showing the blessings and safeguards inherent in God's will for sexual chastity before marriage and faithfulness in marriage; and

7. To teach within our Lutheran schools and churches the biological, social and parental functions of childbearing; and

8. To support the efforts to secure the Human Life Amendment to the United States Constitution.

APPENDIX E.

The following paper was given by the author on September 22, 1979 to the Northern Iowa-Southern Minnesota Circuit Conference of the Evangelical Lutheran Synod.

NATURAL LAW AND ITS IMPORTANCE FOR TWENTIETH CENTURY AMERICA

The concept of natural law is badly neglected today. It is possible, perhaps even probable, that many Americans do not even know what the term "natural law" means. In fact, we would probably be safe in saying that a person could progress educationally all the way to a doctorate degree without being aware of natural law. He may never even hear the word used.

Because there is such widespread ignorance of the natural law concept, we must begin with the most basic of considerations. A starting point could be a discussion of moral law, since understanding natural law goes hand-in-hand with understanding moral law.

WHAT IS THE MORAL LAW?

We can find no better description of the moral law than that which is given in the Bible. The Scriptures also describe a ceremonial law and we must be clear on the difference between the two. The ceremonial law was a temporary system of requirements given to the Old Testament Jews for the purpose of reminding them of the promised Messiah. The moral law, on the other hand, is the universal code of ethics (right and wrong) which stipulates how we are to be — how we should act, think, value, etc. The focus of the moral law is upon mankind and our behavior, while the focus of the ceremonial law was always upon Christ and what he would do. We might say that the ceremonial law was a gospel-oriented sort of code, while the moral law is a human behavior-oriented code. Unfortunately the Jewish teachers of Jesus' day had largely lost the gospel content of the ceremonial law.

The moral law, as we have said, tells us how we are to live. In describing this moral law the Scriptures use two different forms of the moral code. This may surprise us, but that is how the Bible reveals the moral law to us. These two different forms of the moral law actually compliment each other in a way that allows us to understand the moral law in its completeness.

One of the Biblical expressions, perhaps that form with which we are the most familiar, is the Ten Commandments. These Commandments are a masterpiece in the exposition of moral law. They begin with the most basic principle of the law, that of the required honor and respect for God, and proceed to specific standards for protecting the human family, human life and human posessions. These Commandments then end by prohibiting the origin of many destructive actions, namely the sin of coveting. In this way the Commandments include the basic precepts of love to God and man, and at the same time demonstrate how such love and respect must be applied in our lives, beginning with the human heart. These Commandments are unsurpassed in laying out the totality of the moral law in a brief form. We would do well to study each of these Commandments carefully. Luther's *Large Catechism* is an excellent aid for such a study.

But the Commandments are not the only Biblical form of the moral law. The rabbi in Luke chapter 10 was correct when he stated the moral law in this manner: " 'Love the Lord your God with all your heart, with all your soul, with all your strength and with all your mind,' and 'Love your neighbor as yourself.' " He was quoting from Deuteronomy 6:5 and Leviticus 19:18. Jesus himself described the moral law in the same fashion in Matthew 22:37,38. We can see from such statements that the moral law can be summarized in just one word — love. To love God and man is a true and complete expression of the entire moral law. For this reason the moral law can be called the law of love.

What, then, is the relationship between the Ten Commandments and the law of love? They are simply two ways of saying the same thing. If we could love God and man perfectly, then our behavior would match each of the Commandments. Similarily, if we could fulfill every Commandment perfectly, we would do so only out of perfect love. The word love gets at the basic condition of the human heart, while the Commandments show both the necessity of such love and how that love will apply itself in our daily lives. St. Paul states this well in Romans 13:9,10: "The Commandments, 'Do not commit adultery,' 'Do not murder,' 'Do not steal,' 'Do not covet,' and whatever other commandment there may be, are summed up in this one rule: 'Love your neighbor as yourself.' Love does no harm to its neighbor. Therefore love is the fulfillment of the law."

A diagram is useful at this point:

THE MORAL LAW

<u>Ten Commandments</u>   Law of Love

This sketch intends to show that a balanced understanding of the moral law demands that both forms of expression be clearly recognized. The balance is extremely important and if the balance is lost, a perversion of the moral law can only result. For example, the well-known philosopher in the field of ethics, Joseph Fletcher, puts the two sides of the balance in opposition to each other. He says that the Commandments are legalistic and that we are not bound by them but are only bound by the law of love. He then applies his views in such a way as to argue that it is an act of love to kill unwanted babies by abortion and to eliminate defective newborn infants, and to provide merciful deaths to the hopelessly ill.[1] This is what can happen when the Commandments are denied — murder becomes defined as a loving act! What could be more diabolical than this? A basic truth that should be making itself more and more clear to us is that whenever the moral law is diminished in any way, the result is the exploitation of those of us who are defenseless. Evil is real and must be restrained. Otherwise the vulnerable will suffer the consequences.

The opposite extreme from Fletcher's view is the legalistic emphasis of the Commandments and other codes to the exclusion of the law of love. The Pharisees of Jesus' time fell into this trap. By forgetting about genuine love for God and man, and by making the Commandments into a superficial system of exter-

90

nals, these hypocrites thought they could satisfy the demands of the moral code and thus earn eternal life. Actually all these moralizers did was channel the desires of their evil hearts into technically legal, but totally destructive acts of exploitation towards the needy. How accurately Jesus told them that they were extremely concerned about trivial externals, and at the same time they devoured widows' houses. There is no keeping of the law without the heart being right. Jesus, in his Sermon on the Mount, hammered away at these legalists, trying to get them to think in terms of hatred, lust, greed, envy and the like as being the genuine concerns of the law. Jesus pointed them to the human heart because that is what they had missed.

To properly understand the moral law, therefore, the double emphasis of the Ten Commandments and the law of love must be maintained. If we diminish either side of the balance, the moral code will be lost to at least some degree. When we fully appreciate both modes of expression, however, then we will begin to grasp how broad and how disconcertingly exacting this moral code is. This code is nothing less than the expression of everything that God expects of us. Let us also keep in mind that a major purpose of the moral code is to drive us to Christ by showing us our sinfulness. When we understand the moral law, our sorry moral state is a foregone conclusion. Thanks be to Christ for giving us the victory!

WHAT IS NATURAL LAW?

Nature has two kinds of laws. One type, the kind of law of nature with which we are probably the most familiar, is the system of regular patterns governing the properties of nature's elements and forces. These are the laws of the chemist, the physicist and the biologist. The second type of law possessed by nature is the sense of right and wrong naturally possessed by all mankind. The first type of law mentioned is commonly called the law(s) of nature. This type of law will be ignored for the rest of this study. The second type of law is commonly called natural law, because it is part of the common (natural) knowledge of all persons, and because it is that system of morality (moral law) which governs the rightness or wrongness of all human actions. Hence the name "natural law."

Natural law is part of our common knowledge in two complimentary ways. In the first place, natural law is part of our instinctive knowledge. Let us observe, by way of analogy, the intricate nest built by the Baltimore oriole. This nest is a marvel of both design and construction, yet the oriole never learned how to build such a nest. This nest-building knowledge is possessed by the oriole because it was conceived an oriole. The knowledge is totally instinctive, transmitted through the oriole genes. Similarly, natural law does not have to be learned by mankind, it is an instinctive knowledge that is ours by virtue of our conception as human beings. St. Paul states this truth clearly in Romans 2:15: ". . . since they show that the requirements of the law are written on their hearts. . . ." Paul then proceeds to argue that man's conscience demonstrates that this moral law is really there. Since many such people have never been taught the revealed moral law, the Commandments of the Bible, this universal awareness of right and wrong testifies to the reality of the instinctive natural law. This is Paul's argument.

It is interesting that modern psychological research has discovered the same truth. Lawrence Kohlberg of Harvard University is considered our nation's most prominent psychologist in the field of morals. Dr. Kohlberg has done extensive experimentation which reveals that all people have an awareness of right and wrong, and that this awareness results from certain underlying moral premises. Kohlberg has concluded that even though some people progress farther than others in realizing these basic moral premises, nevertheless, the moral values are constant in all cultures.[2] Actually Kohlberg never "discovered" this truth, because the Bible and the Lutheran confessions state these things clearly. But Kohlberg is the first to have demonstrated in a scientific way that natural law is real. His brilliant work in this field has brought him to his current position of prominence.

There is yet a second avenue for the realization of the precepts of natural law. Instinct, as we have noted, is the first avenue. This second manner of realizing natural law derives from our natural knowledge of God by virtue of inescapable reasoning. Let us begin with the natural knowledge of God. Paul explains in Romans chapter one that God has revealed himself to all men through the glory of his creation. Specifically Paul states (Romans 1:19,20): ". . . since what may be known about God is plain to them, because God has made it plain to them. For since the creation of the world God's invisible qualities — his eternal power and divine nature — have been clearly seen, being understood from what has been made, so that men are without excuse." In this way Paul makes it clear that God's existence can be logically inferred from nature.

Philosophers have been studying the ways our minds conclude the existence of God from nature; they have been studying and debating this process for thousands of years. Essentially we must observe that there is an intricate and masterful design which is built into all of nature and that there must be some causal force behind such a world. Martin Luther explained this natural knowledge of God in a sermon given on October 20, 1537. Says Luther: "They are all acquainted with the law of nature. The Gentiles are all aware that murder, adultery, theft, cursing, lying, deceit and blasphemy are wrong. They are not so stupid that they do not know very well that there is a God who punishes such vices. Furthermore, their reason tells them that the heavenly bodies cannot run their definite course without a ruler."[3] Because this knowledge of God's existence is logically concluded from a sutdy of nature, it is called the natural knowledge of God.

This natural knowledge of God is of utmost importance, but we must also recognize its limitations. This logical process can tell us that God is, but it can never tell us the qualities of God that we need to know most. It can never tell us that God is triune, or that the creation was out of nothing, and most importantly it can never tell us the gospel of Christ. The gospel comes only through the Word and Sacraments of baptism and communion. Accordingly the Lutheran confessions refer to the natural knowledge of God as being a "dim spark" which can never bring us back to fellowship with God. In a day when the Church of Rome has elevated the natural knowledge of God to saving status (Second Vatican Council) it is of utmost importance that we maintain that faith comes by hearing the Word of God alone, and that salvation comes through Christ alone.

But even though the natural knowledge of God cannot lead men to the gospel, it does drive them to a deeper awareness of right and wrong. If someone has made us, it is only logical that he must have some expectations for our lives. If he has made the rest of the world, it must have value and ought not lightly be destroyed. If he has made man as the crown of creation, then mankind must deserve the best protection of all. In this fashion the moral codes can be deduced from the existence of God. Conversely, if there is no God, then we can set our own moral standards and can set them any way we wish to. Right and wrong then cease to be absolutes and become nothing more than the conventions of society. The recognition of God and the recognition of genuine right and wrong always go together. Tom Hardt aptly describes this relationship between the natural knowledge of God and natural law as follows: "...the concept of natural law is in principle extended by the concept of the natural knowledge of God: the law presupposes the law-giver and without the law-giver there is no law."[4]

Let us also remember that natural law includes both tables of the law — that is, our duties to God as well as to our fellow men. We cannot honor God without recognizing his existence, and similarily we can only conclude that he deserves our utmost honor when we realize that he does exist. For both tables of the law, law-giver and law must go hand-in-hand. And both instinct and human reason based on creation will enable mankind to realize the precepts of natural law.

WHAT IS THE RELATIONSHIP BETWEEN THE MORAL LAW AS REVEALED IN THE BIBLE AND NATURAL LAW?

Perhaps it is clear by this time that the content of moral law and natural law are one and the same. The term "natural law" simply refers to the manner in which the law has been learned. This concept in no way changes the content of the moral law. In case this principle might be questioned, let us briefly consider three reasons for agreeing that the precepts of moral law and natural law are the same.

(1) In Romans 1 and 2 Paul discusses the moral law as revealed to the Jews in the Scriptures, along with natural law. Never does Paul suggest that there is any difference in the content. Law (Greek νόμος) is always a singular concept in Romans. Even though there are many demands in this moral law, the code itself is a unit. Specifically Paul says that: "Indeed when the Gentiles,

who do not have the law, do by nature things required by the law, they are a law for themselves." (Romans 2:14) In this way Paul shows that the moral codes the heathen are instinctively following are the same moral codes as are revealed in the Bible. More was expected of the Jews because of the great advantage they had by virtue of the Scriptures, yet the moral codes described are one and the same. Christians too have a moral code which is no different from that of the non-Christians. We have tremendous advantages in understanding these standards and living according to them, but the precepts themselves are the same.

(2) If we compare the content of the moral law to the content of natural law, we will see that they are the same. An excellent expression of natural law is the Golden Rule: "Do unto others as you would have them do unto you." The precept so described is the same as that in the words of Jesus: "Love your neighbor as yourself." (Matthew 22:39).

(3) Thirdly, the Lutheran confessions treat the contents of both laws as being the same. In fact, in his exposition of the Third Commandment in the *Large Catechism* Luther actually appeals to natural law to determine that a specific day for worship is no longer required. Worship need not be on the Sabbath. But, says Luther, "nature teaches" a day of rest is necessary for all working people. Luther is here assuming natural law and moral law to have the same content, and on that basis he can appeal to natural law for the correct understanding of the moral law.

In summary we have seen that all persons have the same moral principles in their hearts. Most people have these precepts by virtue of their instinct and reason alone, while some have the additional advantage of God's revealed Word. Let us now turn to the importance of this knowledge of the moral law.

THE IMPORTANCE OF NATURAL LAW

Natural law has three functions or uses. They are: (1) To provide a firm guideline for social and political life and thereby protect the innocent and restrain the powers of evil; (2) To show us our sinfulness and thereby drive us to Christ; (3) To enable all persons individually to understand the difference between good and evil and thereby to demonstrate how to live a virtuous life.

If we apply natural law to the work of the church, it quickly becomes apparent that in congregational life we are most interested in the second and third of these uses of the law. Since the purpose of the church is to preach the gospel of Christ, the law must also be taught so that people realize their need for the gospel. But we also know that the gospel produces fruits of faith, and this same law must be proclaimed so that Christians know how to channel their Christian love into productive activities. The church's primary function is not to involve itself with purely social or political questions, but has the obligation of showing its membership how to live out the love of Christ in the social and political world.

The church can find itself caught in either of two unfortunate extremes. The one is to preach politics and social issues instead of the gospel. The other is to neglect its proper role of teaching the third use of the law in such a way that it can be rightly applied in one's daily life, including one's political and social life. Either extreme is ultimately a denial of the gospel of Christ.

If we apply natural law to the work of the state, it becomes apparent that here the political use of the law is the most important. Let us also bear in mind that as Christians we live in both the church and the state and we have major obligations to both spheres. The purpose of government is none other than the maintenance of good order so that all are protected and honest endeavors may flourish. And what is the foundation for this work of the state? It is nothing other than natural law. God himself has set up government and bestowed upon it the right to govern. Consequently the state is obligated to follow God's own principles of good order.

This governmental power is recognized in the Fourth Commandment, in addition to its being instinctive to all men. We must also insist that according to the Fourth Commandment God has given the primary governing authority to parents; the right of the state is, therefore, derived from the rights of parents. Luther explains this principle in the *Large Catechism* when he says: "Out of the authority of parents all other authority is derived and developed." Speaking hypothetically, if a group of people found themselves isolated in a remote area of the globe, some form of government would be necessary for good order. If that group of people were a family of parents and children, the form of government would already be set. If the group were in time to grow beyond a single family, then some of the parental rights would have to be delegated for good order. This is basically how it works. This also means that the parents' rights as parents supersede the rights of the state. The government has over-stepped its bounds if in any way it abrogates parents' rights over their children, or if the state mitigates any other familial rights.

Since the right to govern rests on natural law, the standards of the state must follow natural law. The state never has a right to act contrary to natural law, but must always follow the moral law's precepts closely. The Lutheran Confessions act on this principle when they state: "Now since natural right is unchange-able, the right to contract marriage must always remain" (Apolo-gy of the Augsburg Confession, Article XXIII). In this way the confessors contend that it would be unjust for any body, govern-mental or otherwise, to deny the right of marriage because that right is guaranteed by natural law. Just a few lines earlier this confession appealed to Emperor Charles that he enact laws governing marriage which would comply with natural law.

This is the correct posture of the Christian before the state. We must show what natural law requires and then we must argue that the state is required to follow these precepts. The love of Christ will compel us to act in this way. No Christian, whether clergy-man or layman, has the liberty or privilege of sitting quietly back when natural law is being denied and the helpless are being exploited as a result. The love of Christ constrains us to speak out loudly and clearly to the state while showing to all what is right and wrong morally, and showing that all governments must follow these moral law principles in so far as is possible.

When Christians speak out in this way, it is often alleged that we are trying to force our moral values on those of differing religious persuasions. Nothing could be further from the truth. As has been demonstrated, the Christian's understanding of mo-ral law is no different from the basic understanding of all people. We have some advantage, both in knowing the details and in being able to follow this law in part. Nevertheless, the law we proclaim is universal and common to all men. The wicked may suppress the law to a large degree, but they can never escape it. Their conscience will always bear this out.

As Americans we have been extremely fortunate that our country was founded squarely on natural law. The Declaration of Independence leaves no doubt about this at all by stressing that our rights derive from "nature" and "nature's God." The first right then specified as deriving from nature and nature's God is the right to life. Our Constitution was built on these noble precepts, with the Bill of Rights included as a guarantee that our natural law rights would never be disavowed. When we Christians, therefore, insist that our nation follow the basic natural law principles, we are not only standing on the fundamental principle of all good government, we are also standing on the most basic premises of our nation specifically. It is because of its natural law foundation that our country has become a shining example of freedom and equal protection under the law. As this base is being eroded, however, our basic human rights are disappearing.

THE DENIAL OF NATURAL LAW

This section could also be called the destruction of social order, because to deny natural law is to destroy the social order. It is becoming increasingly obvious that our nation is straying further and further away from recognizing and following natural law, and as a direct result our rights are increasingly being denied and the helpless are increasingly being exploited.

A good analysis of the moral and social revolution occuring in our nation is given by Harold O. J. Brown in his *Human life Review* article called "What Makes the Law the Law?"[5] Brown shows that Western civilization has always regarded the law as something to be discovered, not something to be made. That is, given the fact that government is based on natural law and given the fact that natural law is unchangeable, then the making of civil laws is a process of clarifying natural law and applying those principles to the particular situation of the country. But now, due to the influence of evolutionary theory and humanistic philosophy, many modern legislators and judges view law as something to be created in such a way as to follow society's current values. Essentially this new approach sees man as the creator of the law instead of God.

Using this new approach (often called social contract theory) a given country could set its standards for right and wrong along any lines whatsoever. For example, if a society agrees that abortion is right, then it is seen as morally right. Similarily, if a society decrees that homosexual marriage is morally right, then it too is seen as a positive moral good. Using this diabolical theory, murder and all manners of perversion become defined as right and loving acts. Satan always strives to turn the truth upside down, to make white black and black white. This is precisely what the new approach to civil law does. Following this new philosophy, we could never say that any right is absolute or "unalienable," since society could change anything. The government of necessity becomes then the arm of society, and practically speaking it is really the decisions of government that become the absolute right in the land. It always works this way — if human rights are not absolute, then in some form government becomes absolute.

This is why many of our policies, like abortion for example, now are no different from the policies of the Soviet Union. If there is no natural law, then ultimately anything goes. And if there are no absolute human rights, then there are no human rights at all. We come under the mercy of an arbitrary government that has no restraint upon it.

This new approach to law is well illustrated by the Humanist Manifesto II. This document begins with a denial of God's existence and with a denial of natural law. The document then asserts that right and wrong are totally situational concepts. Following consistently from these premises, the Manifesto ignores all the basic rights, such as the right to life, and emphasizes instead that we have the right to abortion, suicide, divorce and homosexual practice. The sequence of thought follows precisely the description given by Paul in Romans 1 where he explains that the denial of God leads to all manner of destructive and perverted behavior. If we read Romans 1-2, we will see that Paul's description of the totally corrupted life-style reads distressingly like the current American social and moral scene as revealed in any of the newspapers.

To make matters worse American schools are widely advocating this humanistic way of thinking with its denial of natural law. Lawrence Kohlberg has effectively reprimanded the schools for their foolish statements that they are not teaching morality. Kohlberg demonstrates that there is a large hidden moral curriculum taught in the schools, a curriculum that shows up clearly, says Kohlberg, in such places as sex education. (The Manifesto itself states that sex education is a primary avenue for teaching its brand of moral reasoning.)

Clearly the denial of natural law has had a devastating effect on our nation. In her speech entitled, "Is the New Morality Destroying America?" Clare Boothe Luce demonstrates that our new view of ethics is producing the uncontrolled upsurge in such things as abortion, divorce, cohabitation, alcoholism and drug addiction, pornography, homosexuality, prostitution and other crime.[7] Without natural law we simply have no basis for good social order. We may not care to admit this fact, but the destruction of our nation is being carried out before our own eyes.

WHAT CHRISTIANS MUST DO

The only way that justice and order can be revitalized in our nation is by a return to natural law as the basis for government. This will not be an easy task, since natural law has been repressed for many years and humanistic ideology has become deeply entrenched in many of our national institutions, especially the schools. But natural law is part of the nature of mankind, so it can never be completely destroyed. Even in the Communist countries the recognition of genuine right and wrong keeps coming up.

We Christians, who are the salt of the earth, who live in both the churchly and governmental kingdoms, who are compelled by the love of Christ to help our fellow men in whatever way we can, and who know so clearly the difference between good and evil, absolutely must lead the way in bringing our nation back to its moral consciousness. It is not surprising that we find the Christians in the forefront of the battles over immoral governmental actions. We Christians have the love of Christ. We cannot do otherwise. Most of the needy who have been robbed of their possessions and left to die are not lying on our nation's highways, however. We can be Good Samaritans in our day only by actively using the political process. The theft and murder are being done in the political arena. Then this arena is where we must work. We have no other choice.

Christ has left us his work to do. We are his hands, we are his spokesmen, we are his witnesses. Let us be mindful of the great effort Jesus made to befriend those who were in need. If we do otherwise, we have denied our Christianity. We know that we have been saved by faith alone in Christ. But we know also that Christ has given us his work to do. In the church proper this work is the preaching of both law and gospel. In the state this work is protecting and sustaining those in need. We do not know how much success we will have, but we know that God will bless our efforts. We speak only the truth, and when we champion the precepts of natural law, everyone in his heart knows we are speaking that truth.

Let us go forward. May God bless our efforts, and may God use us to extend his protecting hand to all who are in need.

NOTES TO APPENDIX E

1. Joseph Fletcher and John Warwick Montgomery, *Situation Ethics,* Dimension Books, Minneapolis, 1972, pp. 13-25.
2. Lawrence Kohlberg, "The Claim to Moral Adequacy of a Highest Stage of Moral Judgement," *The Journal of Philosophy,* Volume 70, Oct. 25, 1973, pp. 630-647.
3. *Luther's Works,* American Edition, Concordia Publishing House, St. Louis, Vol. 22, p. 149.
4. Tom Hardt, "Natural Knowledge of God and Natural Law According to the Teaching of the Evangelical Lutheran Church," *The Lutheran Synod Quarterly,* Vol. XIX, No. 2, June, 1979, p. 21.
5. Harold O. J. Brown, "What Makes the Law the Law?" *The Human Life Review,* Vol. V, No. 1, Winter, 1979, pp. 68-79.
6. Sara Sanborn, "Means and Ends: Moral Development and Moral Education, *Harvard Graduate School of Education Bulletin,* Fall, 1971.
7. Clare Boothe Luce, "Is the New Morality Destroying America?" *The Human Life Review,* Vol. IV, No. 3, Summer, 1978, pp. 4-16.

END NOTES

1. *Time*, July 9, 1979, pp. 26-27.

2. *Ibid.*

3. This number is given in the same issue of *Time*. Since the Center for Disease Control and the Alan Guttmacher Institute give roughly similar figures, the number is probably reasonably accurate. The Population Council Public Information Office in New York estimates there were 1,270,000 legal abortions 1977.

4. Dorothy Nortman, "Changing Contraceptive Patterns: A Global Perspective," *Population Bulletin*, Vol. 32, No. 3 (Population Reference Bureau, Inc., Washington D.C., 1977), p. 26.

5. *Ibid.*, p. 28.

6. John W. Klotz, *A Christian View of Abortion*, (St. Louis: Concordia Publishing House, 1973), pp. 10-11.

7. Center for Disease Control: Abortion Surveillance, H.E.W. publication No. (CDC)74-8205, issued April 1974.

8. Alex Barno, M.D., *Proposed Constitutional Amendments on Abortion*, "Hearings before the Subcommittee on Civil and Constitutional Rights of the Committee on the Judiciary, House of Representatives, Ninety-fourth Congress," (Washington D.C., U.S. Govt. Printing Office, 1976, Part 2), p. 294.

9. "The Abortion Culture," *Newsweek*, July 9, 1973, p.7.

10. Klotz, *A Christian View of Abortion*, p. 12.

11. These totals are from a variety of sources, including The Alan Guttmacher Institute, and the Center for Disease Control.

12. *Information Please Almanac*, 1979, 33 ed. (The statistics are taken from this source, the chart is constructed by the author based on the statistics.)

13. Robert Destro includes this quotation from the A.M.A. in the *California Law Review*, 1975, Vol. 63:1250, p. 1279. (Reprinted in *Proposed Constitutional Amendments on Abortion*, p. 730.)

14. Destro, *Proposed Constitutional Amendments on Abortion*, p. 729.

15. Bob Woodward and Scott Armstrong, *The Brethren*, (New York: Simon and Schuster, 1979), p. 233.

16. John T. Noonen Jr., *A Private Choice: Abortion in America in the Seventies*, (New York: The Free Press, 1979), p. 32.

17. *Ibid.*

18. George Kaluger and Meriem Kaluger, (St. Louis: The C.V. Mosby Company, 1979), pp. 65-66.

19. Elizabeth Hall, Ed., (New York: Random House, Inc., 3rd ed., 1979) p. 75.

20. James Lugo and L. Hershey, *Human Development*, (Macmillan Publishing Co., Inc., 1979), pp. 288-290.

21. Courtesy of the Population Reference Bureau, Inc., In Brewer, "Abortion: the Continuing Controversy," (Washington D.C., *Population Bulletin*, August, 1972, Vol. 28, No. 4) p. 20.

22. As quoted by Senator James Buckley from *The New England Journal of Medicine*, contained in *Proposed Constitutional Amendments on Abortion*, p. 678.

23. *Proposed Constitutional Amendments on Abortion*, p. 677.

24. The name "Jane Doe" is a pseudonym. The article is as reprinted by Minnesota Citizens Concerned for Life (MCCL). Used by permission of the Associated Press.

25. *California Medicine*, September, 1970, Vol. 113, No. 3, pp. 67-68.

26. As quoted by Jeanne Head, RN., in *Proposed Constitutional Amendments on Abortion*, p. 934.

27. *Ibid*, p. 641.

28. C. Everett Koop, *The Right to Live; The Right to Die*, (Wheaton; Tyndale House Publishers, Inc., 1976), p. 48.

29. Brewer, "Abortion: the Continuing Controversy," p. 8.

30. Nortman, "Changing Contraceptive Patterns: A Global Perspective," p. 28.

31. Reprinted in the appendix of *Proposed Constitutional Amendments on Abortion*, pp. 944-945.

32. *Time*, "Wondering if Children are Necessary," March 5, 1979, pp. 42-43.

33. Statistics from *Information Please Almanac*, 1979, 33 ed.

34. As defined by the United Nations, Dept. of Economic and Social affairs. Definition is contained in Nortman, "Changing Contraceptive Patterns: A Global Perspective, *Population Bulletin*, No. 3, August 1977, p. 32.

35. These figures are of 1972. From the *Medical World News*, Oct., 1973. Reprinted in *Proposed Constitutional Amendments on Abortion*, pp. 949-950.

36. *Ibid.*

37. Archibald Cox, *The Role of the Supreme Court in American Government*, (New York: Oxford University Press, 1976), p. 52.

38. Representative John Y. McCollister from Nebraska, *Proposed Constitutional Amendments on Abortion*, p. 647.

39. Senator James Buckley from New York, *Ibid.*, p. 677.

40. *California Medicine*, September, 1970, Vol. 113, No. 3, pp. 67-68.

41. As stated to the Senate on May 31, 1973, given as quoted by Al Quie in *Proposed Constitutional Amendments on Abortion*, p. 655.

42. Sara Sanborn, "Means and Ends: Moral Development and Moral Education, *Harvard Graduate School of Education Bulletin*, Fall, 1971.

43. Reported in a brochure by Minnesota citizens Concerned for Life (MCCL).

44. *The Human Life Review*, Vol. IV, No. 3, Summer of 1978.

45. John T. Noonan, Jr., *A Private Choice: Abortion in America in the Seventies*, p. 46.

46. Proposed Constitutional Amendments on Abortion, pp. 583-584.

47. *Christian News*, July 16, 1979, p. 16.

BIBLIOGRAPHY

The following selected works are recommended for further information concerning the abortion revolution:

Brown, Harold O. J. *Death before Birth*. Nashville: Thomas Nelson Inc., 1977.

Human Life Review. Published quarterly at 150 East 35th Street, New York, N.Y., 10016.

Koop, C. Everett. *The Right to Live; the Right to Die*. Wheaton: Tyndale House Publishers, 1976.

Lewis, C. S. *That Hideous Strength*. New York: The Macmillan Company, 1946.

Lewis, C.S. *The Abolition of Man*. New York: The Macmillan Company, 1947.

Noonan, John T. Jr. *A Private Choice: Abortion in America in the Seventies*. New York: The Free Press, 1979.

Proposed Constitutional Amendments on Abortion. "Hearings before the Subcommittee on Civil and Constitutional Rights, of the Committee on the Judiciary, House of Representatives, Ninety-fourth Congress, Second Session, February 4, 5, March 22, 23, 24, 25 and 26, 1976." Serial No. 46, Parts 1 and 2. U.S. Government Printing Office, Washington D.C. 20402.

Ramsey, Paul. *Ethics at the Edges of Life*. New Haven and London: Yale University Press, 1978.

Schaeffer, Francis A. *How Should We Then Live? The Rise and Decline of Western Thought and Culture*. Old Tappan, New Jersey: Fleming H. Revell Company, 1976. (The same content is also available in the 10 part film series by the same title.)

Schaeffer, Francis A. and C. Everett Koop. *Whatever Happened to the Human Race?* Old Tappan, New Jersey: Fleming H. Revell Company, 1979. (Also available as a film series under the same title.)

Teigen, Bjarne W. *The Lutheran Doctrine of the Two Kingdoms and its significance for the American Bicentennial.* 1975 Reformation Lectures, October 30 and 31, 1975, Bethany Lutheran College, Mankato, Minnesota, 56001.

Teigen, Erling and Allen Quist. *The Sanctity of Human Life.* A pamphlet containing reprints of articles in the *Lutheran Sentinel* on January 11, 1979 and January 25, 1979. Available at Lutheran Synod Book Company, 734 Marsh St., Mankato, MN 56001.

Warnke, Harold. *Abortion.* Northwestern Publishing House, Milwaukee, 1980.

Wilke, Dr. and Mrs. J.C. *Handbook on Abortion.* Cincinnati; Hiltz, 1971.

Woodward, Bob and Scott Armstrong. *The Brethren: Inside the Supreme Court.* New York; Simon and Schuster, 1979.